Patterns of Suicide and Homicide in the World

Patterns of Suicide and Homicide in the World

David Lester

Nova Science Publishers, Inc.
New York

Art Director: Maria Ester Hawrys
Assistant Director: Elenor Kallberg
Graphics: Susan Boriotti and Frank Grucci
Manuscript Coordinator: Phylis Gaynor
Book Production: Gavin Aghamore, Joanne Bennette,
Michele Keller, Christine Mathosian
and Tammy Sauter
Circulation: Iyatunde Abdullah, Cathy DeGregory and
Annette Hellinger

Library of Congress Cataloging–in–Publication Data
available upon request

ISBN 1-56072-392-0

6080 Jericho Turnpike, Suite 207
Commack, New York 11725
Tele. 516-499-3103 Fax 516-499-3146
E Mail Novasci1@aol.com

Printed in the United States of America

CONTENTS

CHAPTER 1.

Introduction 1

CHAPTER 2.

The validity of national rates of suicide and homicide 7

CHAPTER 3.

The collection of the suicide and homicide rates of nations of the world 25

CHAPTER 4.

The choice of the sample 35

CHAPTER 5.

A correlational analysis 45

CHAPTER 6.

Predicting national suicide and homicide rates 59

CHAPTER 7.

National differences in lethal violence 65

CHAPTER 8.

Changes in suicide and homicide rates 71

CHAPTER 9.

Changes in the methods used for suicide from 1960 to 1980 75

CHAPTER 10.

Gender differences in suicide and homicide rates **81**

CHAPTER 11.

Trends in suicide from 1970 to 1984 .... **91**

CHAPTER 12.

A critical-mass theory of suicide and homicide rates **97**

CHAPTER 13.

Suicide and homicide across the lifespan **103**

CHAPTER XIV.

Suicide, homicide and the quality of life **127**

CHAPTER XV.

Murdering babies **135**

CHAPTER XVI.

Time-series analyses, 1950-1985 .... **141**

CHAPTER XVII.

Conclusions **157**

Subject Index **159**

CHAPTER 1

INTRODUCTION

This book examines (and tries to account for) the variation in the suicide and homicide of the nations of the world. When people are asked to guess which nation has the highest suicide rate, most people guess that either Sweden or Japan has the highest rate. When they are told that Hungary has the highest suicide rate, they are intrigued. The first question they ask is "Why?"

I have faced that question many times and had no idea how to answer it. There have been two approaches in the efforts to answer such a question. In the first approach, a clinical strategy, an investigator becomes familiar with one culture and writes a paper explaining why the culture has the suicide rate that it has or why the suicides are of a particular type. Hendin (1965) has done this for Denmark, Norway and Sweden, and Iga (1986) has done this for Japan. However, few countries have been examined in this way, and it has not been possible to achieve consistency by having just one investigator examine a large sample of countries. Hendin's study of three represents the most countries examined by a single investigator. Furthermore, the approach suffers from questions of validity. There is no sound way to check the validity of the observer's conclusions about the nature of the culture under investigation.

The second approach has been statistical. Suicide and homicide rates are collected for a sample of nations of the world, and these rates are correlated with one or more social characteristics of the nations. For example, Stack (1983) found that the suicide rates of 25 nations were associated with measures of religious commitment (percentage of books published that are religious), industrialization (the gross national product per capita), and gender equality in the labor force.

One problem with these studies is that often the sample of nations studied is quite small since data are not available for a large sample either for rates of personal violence or for the social characteristics. Furthermore, most investigators study only a very small number of social characteristics.

THE GOALS OF THIS BOOK

The first goal in the present study is to collect rates of personal violence (suicide and homicide) for as large a sample of nations as possible. This will permit the testing of psychological and sociological hypotheses concerning national rates of personal violence on an adequate sample.

A second goal is to collect data on a wide variety of social characteristics of nations rather than a few. These social characteristics will, of course, be correlated with the suicide and homicide rates of the nations. But, in addition, these social characteristics will be factor-analyzed to identify clusters of related social characteristics. Then scores of the nations on these clusters will be correlated with the national rates of personal violence to better identify which cultural characteristics are related to the rates of personal violence. Studies using statistical methods for determining the relationship among quantified variables across cultures are called hologeistic studies (Shaefer, 1977), and the particular type of analysis proposed here is called an ecological factor analysis.

The present study will, of course, benefit from all of the earlier studies on national rates of personal violence, and we will be able to explore whether these previous studies can be replicated using the present sample of nations.

EARLIER ECOLOGICAL STUDIES OF NATIONAL CHARACTERISTICS

Before we proceed with the study, we must acknowledge that several studies have been conducted in the past to explore ways in which nations differ and to identify different clusters of social characteristics. Let us first describe the results of a few of these studies.

One of the first cross-cultural studies of modern nations was conducted by Banks and Textor (1963) who collected data on 57 variables for 115 nations. They presented a computer print-out of 1257 pages in which each of the 57 characteristics was cross-tabulated with every other characteristic.

These characteristics were factor analyzed by Gregg and Banks (1965) who identified seven factors, three of which explained 51 percent of the variance in the data: multiparty systems of government versus one-party systems, old and westernized versus young and ex-colonial, and stable versus unstable regimes.

Adelman and Morris (1967) have also examined sociocultural, political and economic indicators for a sample of developing nations, as have Cattell (Cattell, 1949; Cattell, et al., 1952; Cattell and Gorsuch, 1965), Rummel (1972), Russett (1968), Sawyer (1967).

Lynn (1971) restricted his sample to the eighteen most industrialized nations in the free world and set himself the goal of trying to measure differences in the national character of the citizens in these nations by using objective indices. In the final version, Lynn used twelve variables: chronic psychosis, calorie intake, caffeine consumption, coronary heart disease, alcoholism, suicide, murder, crime, divorce, cigarette consumption, illegitimacy and accidents (Lynn and Hampson, 1977). Factor analysis revealed two components which Lynn labelled anxiety/neuroticism and extraversion based upon the results of psychological research linking these twelve behaviors to personality. Each nation in the sample was given a score for each of the components.

Interestingly for our present purpose is that suicide was included among the characteristics which measured anxiety/neuroticism while murder was included among those which measured extraversion.

Alcock and Eckhardt (1974) measured a characteristic of nations which they called compassion. They used a sample of 52 nations and various indices such as the absence of civil violence, health and education, equality, international cooperation, and freedom of the press, to score these nations for this trait and to rank them in order.

Estes (1984) has been concerned with the quality of life in modern nations, and he has used 44 welfare-relevant social indicators, grouped into eleven major areas, to measure the quality of life in each nation. His variables include for example, percent adult illiteracy (in the education index), male life expectancy (in the health status index), and number of major disasters (in the geography index).

Stewart and Winter (1977) were interested in female inequality and used twenty-five social indicators to measure female status in all available nations of the world. They derived two indices of female status (social-educational equality and economic equality) and one index which they labelled impulse control. They provided scores for each nation of the world for each of the two measures of equality.

SUMMARY

The goals of the present study are, therefore, to obtain rates of suicide and homicide for as many nations of the world as possible and, then, to explore which social characteristics of the nations predict these suicide and homicide rates, drawing upon the results and techniques of earlier ecological studies of nations.

REFERENCES

Adelman, I., & Morris, C. T. *Society, politics and economic development*. Baltimore: Johns Hopkins University Press, 1967.

Alcock, N., & Eckhardt, W. An evaluation of compassion among nations. *Peace Research*, 1974, 5(1), 14-22.

Banks, A. S., & Textor, R. B. *A cross-polity survey*. Cambridge, MA: MIT Press, 1963.

Cattell, R. B. The dimensions of culture patterns by factorization of national characters. *Journal of Abnormal & Social Psychology*, 1949, 44, 443-469.

Cattell, R. B., Breul, H., & Hartman, H. P. An attempt at a more refined definition of the cultural dimensions of syntality in modern nations. *American Sociological Review*, 1952, 17, 408-421.

Cattell, R. B., & Gorsuch, R. L. The definition and measurement of national morale and morality. *Journal of Social Psychology*, 1965, 67, 77-96.

Estes, R. J. *The social progress of nations*. New York: Praeger, 1984.

Gregg, P. M., & Banks, A. S. Dimensions of political systems. *American Political Science Review*, 1965, 59, 602-614.

Hendin, H. *Suicide and Scandinavia*. New York: Basic, 1965.

Iga, M. *The thorn in the chrysanthemum*. Berkeley, CA: University of California, 1986.

Lynn, R. *Personality and national character*. Elmsford, NY: Pergamon, 1971.

Lynn, R., & Hampson, S. L. Fluctuations in national levels of neuroticism and extraversion, 1935-1970. *British Journal of Social & Clinical Psychology*, 1977, 16, 131-137.

Rummel, R. J. *The dimensions of nations*. Beverly Hills, CA: Sage, 1972.

Russett, B. M. Delineating international regions. In J. D. Singer (Ed.) *Quantitative international politics*. New York: Free Press, 1968.

Sawyer, J. Dimensions of nations. *American Journal of Sociology*, 1967, 72, 145-172.

Shaefer, J. M. The growth of hologeistic studies 1889-1975. *Behavior Science Research*, 1977, 12, 71-108.

Stack, S. The effect of religious commitment on suicide. *Journal of Health & Social Behavior*, 1983, 24, 362-374.

Stewart, A. J., & Winter, D. G. The nature and causes of female suppression. *Signs*, 1977, 2, 531-553.

CHAPTER 2

THE VALIDITY OF NATIONAL RATES OF SUICIDE AND HOMICIDE

There have been many criticisms of the validity of national rates of suicide and homicide (Douglas, 1967). For example, it is argued that coroners and medical examiners in different countries have different criteria for certifying death, criteria affected for example by the cultural values of the coroner and by the type of training he has received. In this chapter we will examine some research conducted to explore the validity of national rates of suicide and homicide.

AGE-STANDARDIZED RATES VERSUS UNSTANDARDIZED RATES

Some nations calculate suicide rates standardized for age, and these are now reported by the World Health Organization. It is of interest to compare the age-standardized rates with the nonstandardized rates to see how similar they are.

Data were obtained from the World Health Organization *Annual Statistics* for nations with a population greater than one million for the year 1982 (the year with the largest sample of nations reporting standardized rates) The data are shown in Table 2.1

Table 2.1 Age-Standardized And Nonstandardized Suicide Rates For 1982

	world standardized	nonstandardized
Austria	22.5	27.6
Belgium	17.1	21.9
Bulgaria	12.0	15.3
Canada	12.9	14.3
Chile	5.9	5.6
Denmark	23.9	29.0
Dominican Republic	3.3	2.3
Germany, West	16.6	21.3
Greece	2.9	3.5
Hungary	33.9	43.5
Japan	14.5	17.4
Kuwait	0.1	0.1
Mexico	1.9	1.6
Netherlands	9.0	10.7
Norway	12.5	14.0
Portugal	7.1	8.4
Puerto Rico	7.9	7.6
Sweden	15.5	19.4
UK: England & Wales	7.0	8.6
USA	10.6	12.2
Yugoslavia	14.0	16.1
mean	**11.96**	**14.30**

The Pearson product-moment correlation between the two sets of rates for the 21 nations was 0.997, close to perfect. A comparison of the rates showed that the mean age-standardized rate was 11.96 per 100,000 per year and the mean nonstandardized rate was 14.30, significantly higher ($t = 4.25$, $df = 20$, two-tailed $p < 0.001$).

Since not all nations report age-standardized rates, conducting the cross-national study using only nations that report age-standardized rates would restrict the sample quite severely. Thus, for the present series of studies, it was decided to use the nonstandardized rates.

Table 2.2 Suicide Rates Before And After Changing Classification Systems

	Successive years			
	ICD8	*ICD8*	*ICD9*	*ICD9*
Australia	11.1	11.2	11.6	11.0
Austria	24.8	25.1	25.7	27.1
Bulgaria	13.6	14.4	13.6	13.6
Canada	14.2	14.8	14.2	14.0
Chile	5.2	5.9	4.9	5.8
France	16.5	17.2	18.7	19.4
Germany, West	22.7	22.2	21.5	20.9
Greece	3.3	2.9	2.9	3.3
Hong Kong	13.9	7.2	13.5	13.5
Hungary	40.3	43.1	44.6	44.9
Ireland	4.6	4.9	5.7	6.3
Israel	6.5	5.6	6.6	6.0
Italy	6.2	6.4	7.0	7.3
Japan	17.9	17.6	18.0	17.6
Netherlands	9.2	9.7	10.4	10.1
New Zealand	11.8	10.3	9.7	10.8
Portugal	9.2	9.7	7.4	7.9
Singapore	9.7	11.4	10.5	11.2
Thailand	5.6	5.5	6.7	7.4
UK: England & Wales	8.0	8.2	8.5	8.8
N Ireland	4.6	4.5	4.9	5.2
Scotland	8.1	8.5	9.6	10.0
USA	13.3	12.5	12.1	11.8
average	12.2	12.1	12.5	12.8
standard deviation	8.3	8.8	9.0	9.0

t-test between two middle columns: $t_{22} = 1.25$ (not significant)

Table 2.3 Homicide Rates Before And After Changing Classification Systems

	Successive years			
	ICD8	*ICD8*	*ICD9*	*ICD9*
Australia	1.9	1.8	1.8	1.9
Austria	1.4	1.3	1.2	1.3
Bulgaria	2.6	2.3	2.5	3.4
Canada	2.6	2.5	2.5	2.1
Chile	2.3	2.5	2.6	3.1
France	1.0	1.0	1.1	1.0
Germany, West	1.2	1.2	1.1	1.2
Greece	0.6	0.7	0.7	0.7
Hong Kong	1.4	1.4	1.0	1.6
Hungary	2.0	2.2	2.3	2.6
Ireland	0.9	0.7	0.9	0.7
Israel	1.4	1.6	1.8	1.8
Italy	1.4	1.4	1.6	1.9
Japan	1.2	1.1	1.0	1.0
Netherlands	0.9	0.8	0.9	0.8
New Zealand	1.8	1.9	1.6	1.3
Portugal	1.5	1.6	1.3	1.2
Singapore	1.6	1.7	1.7	2.3
Thailand	18.3	20.5	25.9	25.1
UK: England & Wales	0.9	1.2	1.1	0.8
N Ireland	14.3	5.7	4.3	4.2
Scotland	1.9	1.5	1.5	1.6
USA	9.2	9.4	9.9	10.5
average	3.1	2.9	3.1	3.1
standard deviation	4.5	4.3	5.3	5.2

t-test between two middle columns: $t_{22} = 0.75$ (not significant)

THE EFFECTS OF CHANGING THE CODE FOR THE CLASSIFICATION OF DEATH

Around 1978, the World Health Organization changed from the 8th to the 9th version for the classification of diseases. Did this change have an impact on the suicide and homicide rates?

The suicide and homicide rates for the two years before a nation changed classification system and the two years after were noted. The data for suicide rates are shown in Table 2.2 and the data for homicide rates in Table 2.3 for 23 nations for which data were available with populations greater than one million.

For suicide rates, the rate went up in 14 nations during the two years prior to the change and in 14 nations during the two years after the change. In the two years bridging the change, the rate went up in 14 nations also.

For homicide rates, the rate went up in 10 nations during the two years prior to the change and in eleven nations during the two years after the change. In the two years bridging the change, the rate went up in ten nations.

Thus, these data indicate that changing the classification system appears to have had no noticeable impact on suicide or homicide rates.

CORONER'S DECISIONS AND SUICIDE RATES [1]

As we noted above, it has often been argued that national suicide rates are not valid because of the different biases of the medical examiners in each nation (Douglas, 1967).

Brooke (1974) reported a study of suicide certification in which coroners from eight countries were given a sample of forty case reports of death. Each coroner was asked to classify each death as natural, accidental, homicide or suicide (or open verdict). For the present book, I calculated the average number of suicide verdicts for each nation and correlated the scores with the suicide rate of the nations in 1971 obtained from the World Health Organization (1974). Suicide rates were avialable for seven of the eight nations (see Table 2.4).

The Spearman rank correlation coefficient was 0.47, but not significantly different from zero. Thus, we cannot conclude on the basis of these data that coroner biases are related to official national suicide rates.

---

[1] This section is based on Lester (1986).

Table 2.4 Suicide Rates And Coroners' Decisions

	national suicide rate	coroners' decisions (number out of 40)
Denmark	24.8	29.0
Ireland	2.7	23.5
Netherlands	8.3	24.5
Norway	8.1	23.0
Switzerland	18.6	22.5
UK: England & Wales	8.1	19.2
USA	11.7	25.0

A Comparison of Interpol and World Health Organization Homicide Rates

Interpol (undated) publishes annual data on crimes committed in nations around the world. However, the data on murder are limited by the fact that Interpol includes attempted murder and murder in the same category, although some (but not all) of the nations do report the percentage of actions that were attempts. The data are shown in Table 2.5.

West Germany, for example, reported 2733 murder/attempted murders to Interpol, of which 68.5 percent were attempts. From this we can infer 858 murders. The murder/attempted murder rate reported to Interpol was 4.44 (per 100,000 per year), from which we can calculate a murder rate of 1.39. In contrast West Germany reported 709 homicides to the World Health Organization and a rate of 1.2.

However, Syria reported 700 murders/attempted murder to Interpol, of which 41 percent were attempts. These numbers give a rate of 7.94 for murder/attempts and 4.68 for murder. In contrast, Syria reported two homicides to the World Health Organization, giving a rate of 0.0.

The overall rates for murder/attempted murder provided to Interpol were positively associated with homicide rates provided to the World health Organization (Pearson r = 0.69). Where possible, the rates provided

Table 2.5 A Comparison Of Interpol And World Health Organization Data Sets For 1980

	Interpol			WHO
	rate of murder/ attempts	*percent attempts*	*corrected rate*	*rate of homicide*
Australia	3.11	19.95	2.49	1.9
Austria	2.18	54.90	0.98	1.2
Bahamas	28.64	58.33	11.93	11.4
Barbados	6.71	-	-	4.0
Canada	5.99	57.00	2.58	2.1
Chile	6.13	7.00	5.70	2.6
Costa Rica	6.46	31.03	4.46	5.8
Denmark	4.51	68.40	1.43	1.3
Egypt	2.21	3.61	2.13	0.9
Finland	5.30	55.10	2.38	3.3
France	3.89	-	-	1.0
Germany, West	4.44	68.60	1.39	1.2
Greece	0.85	19.30	0.69	0.7
Hong Kong	1.75	2.30	1.71	1.6
Hungary	3.45	-	-	2.6
Iceland	0.88	-	-	0.9
Ireland (Eire)	0.59	-	-	0.7
Israel	2.05	-	-	1.8
Japan	1.44	42.80	0.82	1.0
Kuwait	3.02	58.54	1.25	0.9
Norway	0.76	-	-	1.1
New Zealand	2.19	21.70	1.71	1.3
Singapore	2.55	-	-	2.3
Spain	1.16	-	-	1.0
Sri Lanka	5.73	32.04	3.89	2.3
Sweden	4.74	66.00	1.61	1.2
Syria	7.94	41.00	4.68	0.0
UK: England/Wales	1.57	20.00	1.26	0.8
Scotland	1.30	-	-	1.6
N Ireland	23.13	74.00	6.01	4.2
USA	10.00	-	-	10.5
Venezuela	13.52	-	-	12.7

to Interpol were corrected for the percentage of attempts, and these rates were more strongly associated with the rates provided to the World Health Organization (r = 0.87).

Although these correlations are positive, the discrepancies between the two sets of data (from Interpol and from the World Health Organization) are so great as to make combination of the two sets of data inadvisable, despite the fact that the Interpol data on murder include rates from nations who do not report to the World Health Organization.

THE VALIDITY OF NATIONAL SUICIDE RATES: A STUDY OF IMMIGRANTS [2]

Sainsbury and Barraclough (1968) correlated the suicide rates in eleven industrialized nations with the suicide rates of immigrants to the United States from these eleven nations. The correlation was 0.87, indicating that nations with high official suicide rates have emigrants who continue to have high suicide rates after they have emigrated to the United States, even though the criteria used by coroners in the United States may be different from those in the home nations. Sainsbury and Barraclough concluded that differences between official suicide rates for different nations may be valid.

Some recent data lend support to the conclusions of Sainsbury and Barraclough. Kramer, et al. (1972) have reported suicide rates by sex for immigrant groups to the United States. The Spearman rank correlation coefficients between the suicide rates of twelve immigrant groups and the suicide rates of the home nations were 0.89 for the total population, 0.92 for males and 0.75 for females. Thus, the relative comparability of official suicide rates may be reasonably accurate for the suicide rates of each sex.

This conclusion was supported by analysis of data from immigrants to Australia. Whitlock (1971) reported suicide rates by sex of immigrants from sixteen nations to Australia from 1965 to 1967 and Burvill, et al. (1973) for immigrants from 12 nations for 1962 to 1966. The Spearman rank correlation coefficients between the suicide rates for the immigrant groups and the suicide rates of the home nations are again quite high: for males 0.79 (n = 16) and 0.91 (n = 12) and for females 0.79 (n = 16) and 0.84 (n = 12).

---

[2] This section is based on Lester (1980, 1989b).

Table 2.6 Suicide Rates Of Immigrants In The USA And Their Home Nations (All Ages And Both Sexes Combined)

	immigrants to USA	home nation 1962
Austria	32.5	22.4
Canada	17.5	7.2
Czechoslovakia	31.5	20.6
Germany, West	25.7	17.6
Ireland	9.8	1.8
Italy	18.2	5.4
Mexico	7.9	-
Norway	23.7	7.9
Poland	25.2	9.3
Sweden	34.2	18.5
UK: England & Wales	19.2	12.0
USSR	30.2	-

Finally, Dublin (1963) reported suicide rates by sex and age for immigrant groups to the United States in 1959. He noted that many of the rates were based on less than twenty cases and so not very reliable. Nevertheless, the suicide rates by age and sex of these immigrant groups were correlated with the suicide rates by age and sex for the home nations for 1962 (World Health Organization, 1965). The data are shown in Tables 2.6 and 2.7, from which it can be seen that sixteen of the eighteen correlation coefficients are positive, and all nine of the statistically significant correlations are positive. In addition, the correlations that are low tend to be for those groups in which the suicide rate is lowest (namely the younger groups and females) and, thus, where the rates are less reliable.

Table 2.7 Correlations Between The Suicide Rates By Age And Sex In Ten Nations With The Suicide Rates Of Immigrants From Those Nations To The USA

Age	Both Sexes	Males	Females
15-24	0.53	0.15	0.15
25-34	0.33	0.52	0.02
35-44	- 0.28	0.07	- 0.05
45-54	0.84*	0.79*	0.59*
55-64	0.48	0.77*	0.52
65-74	0.90*	0.94*	0.57*
75+	0.84*	0.85*	0.38
all ages	**0.92***	**0.95***	**0.71***

* statistically significant at at least the 5% level.

Although doubts have been raised about the validity of official suicide rates reported by nations, the stability of the rankings of the suicide rates of these nations and of immigrants from these nations to the United States and to Australia suggests that national suicide rates may be comparable.

(It should be noted that these rates are based on immigrants from industrialized nations. Data from other nations of the world may not be as reliable.)

AN EXAMINATION OF COUNTRIES WITH ETHNICALLY MIXED POPULATIONS

One way of validating official suicide rates would be to compare the rates of citizens belonging to different ethnic groups within a single nation.

For example, Smith, et al (1986) compared the suicide and homicide rates of Anglos and Hispanics in five southwestern states in the USA for 1976-1980. The rates are shown below, along with the rates for the USA (in 1980) and Mexico (in 1981) as a whole.

	Anglos	USA (whites) 1980	Hispanics	Mexico 1981
suicide	19.2	12.7	9.0	1.7
homicide	7.9	6.9	20.5	17.5

We can see that Hispanics had lower suicide rates than Anglos in the USA, and Mexicans had lower suicide rates than USA whites. Similarly, Hispanics had higher homicide rates than Anglos, and Mexicans had higher homicide rates than USA whites. Since all the suicides and homicide victims in the USA have American medical examiners, the parallels between the rates of Hispanics and Anglos and the rates of USA whites and Mexicans supports the validity of USA and Mexican official statistics.

Hawaii

Kalish (1968) reported suicide rates for the different ethnic groups in Hawaii in 1959-1965.

Hawaii		National suicide rates 1960	
Hawaian	17.8		
white	12.3	*USA*	10.6
Chinese	12.0	*Taiwan*	15.6
Japanese	9.4	*Japan*	21.6
Filipino	5.5	*Philippines*	0.7

It can be seen that, although Filipinos have the lowest suicide rates both in Hawaii and in their home country, the suicide rates of the three remaining groups in Hawaii are not in the same rank order as in the home nations.

Zimbabwe And South Africa

Lester (1988, 1989a) has reported on suicide rates by ethnic group for Zimbabwe for 1983-1986 and South Africa for 1980.

	South Africa		Zimbabwe		USA (1980)	
suicide						
	whites	13.0	*European*	17.6	*whites*	12.7
	blacks	2.7	*African*	6.9	*blacks*[3]	6.0
	colored	4.4	*colored/ asian*	9.7		
	asian	7.3				
homicide						
	whites	3.8			*whites*	6.9
	blacks	22.2			*blacks*	38.1
	colored	44.0				
	asian	8.1				

It can be seen that suicide is more common in whites in all three countries than in people labelled as black and colored. The Asian group is mainly Indian, and the suicide rate in 1979 to 1981 in India itself was 6.0 and the homicide rate 3.2.

The difference in the suicide rates of whites and blacks in Africa has been confirmed by Rwegellera (1978) in Lusaka, Zambia. Thus, we can conclude that suicide rates among blacks in African nations are low while homicide rates are high.

Israel

Miller (1976) reported the suicide rates in Israel in 1968 of those born in different continents. African Jews are primarily from Algeria, Egypt, Libya, Morocco, Sudan, and Tunisia. Asian Jews are primarily from Afghanistan, China, India, Iran, Iraq, Lebanon, Pakistan, Sri Lanka, Syria, Turkey, and

[3] Blacks in the USA include people labelled both as black and colored in South Africa and Zimbabwe.

both Yemens. The rates of the main ethnic groups in Israel is shown below along with rates of comparable countries.

Suicide rates of Israelis born in		National suicide rates in 1970	
Europe/America	21.3	Poland	12.7
		Bulgaria	13.9
Africa	6.9	Egypt	0.1
Asia	9.7	India	6.0
		Syria	0.4
		Turkey	1.8
Israel	6.1		

It can be seen that the rates of immigrants in Israel are higher than those of people in the home nations, but the rates are in roughly the same rank order.

Singapore

Tan (1984) reported suicide rates in Singapore for 1975 to 1984 for the different ethnic groups, and Chia and Tsoi (1972) did so for 1969-1971:

	Singapore 1969-1971		**Singapore 1975-1984**	**National suicide rates 1980**	
	male	*female*	*total*		*total*
Chinese	12.4	8.9	13.8	**Taiwan**	9.9
Malays	2.2	1.0	1.9	**Malaysia**	-
Indians	10.9	8.7	14.1	**India**	6.0

These data are inconclusive since the suicide rates in Malaysia of Indians and Chinese are so similar.

Conclusions

It can be seen that the suicide and homicide rates of different ethnic groups in countries are sometimes similar in rank order to the suicide rates of those in the home nations. This similarity lends support to the proposal that official suicide and homicide rates are reasonably valid.

The Stability of National Suicide Rates in Europe, 1875-1975 [4]

The stability of national suicide rates is a critical issue for most sociological theories of suicide. The major theories of suicide rely on the temporal stability of the suicide rates of societal groups because the causal variables proposed for suicide do not vary greatly over time. For example, Durkheim (1897) proposed two basic causal variables for suicide: social integration and social regulation. The degree to which the individuals in a society are socially integrated and socially regulated does not typically vary much from year to year. Thus, the use of these variables to explain national suicide rates would be futile if those national suicide rates varied widely from year to year.

Given these considerations, it is interesting to inquire how stable national suicide rates have been over a long period of time. The present analysis compares suicide rates of European nations in the period 1871-1875 (Morselli, 1882) with the suicide rates of those nations in 1975 (World Health Organization, 1977-1980).

Several nations were excluded from the analysis since their boundaries changed considerably over the 100 year period (Austria, Germany and the USA). The remaining nations experienced at most minor changes (Belgium, Denmark, England, Finland, France, Hungary, Ireland, Italy, the Netherlands, Norway, Portugal, Spain, Sweden, and Switzerland). The data are shown in Table 2.8.

Table 2.8 National Suicide Rates In 1875 And 1975

[4] This section is based on Lester (1987).

used in correlation	1875	1975
Belgium	6.8	16.2
Denmark	25.8	24.1
England	6.6	7.5
Finland	3.1	25.0
France	15.0	15.8
Hungary	5.2	38.4
Ireland	1.8	4.7
Italy	3.5	5.6
Netherlands	3.5	8.9
Norway	7.3	9.9
Portugal	1.3	8.5
Spain	1.7	3.9
Sweden	8.1	19.4
Switzerland	19.6	22.5
not used in correlations		
German Austria	21.1	24.1
Cisleithan Austria	7.2	-
Germany	16.7	20.9
USA	3.5	12.7

The suicide rates rose over the 100 year period, from a mean of 7.8 per 100,000 per year (SD = 7.3) to 15.0 (SD = 10.0), a difference that was statistically significant ($t = 2.83$, $df = 13$, one-tailed $p < 0.01$).

The Pearson product-moment correlation between the rates for the two periods was 0.42 ($n=14$, one-tailed $p = 0.07$), which almost reaches statistical significance. Thus, the relative suicide rates showed a moderate degree of consistency during the 100 year period.

This result supports the assumption that national suicide rates are relatively stable and thus suitable as target variables for sociological theories that seek to account for suicide rates. Furthermore, the stability of national suicide rates over such a long period of time argues for their validity, since national certification-of-death procedures would be expected to vary over such a long period.

The Stability of Suicide Rates Over Shorter Periods of Time

We have seen that national suicide rates have remained somewhat stable over a hundred year period. Have they remained more stable over shorter periods of time?

Table 2.9 National Suicide Rates At Three Time Periods

	1910-1914	1926-1930	1960
Australia	12.8	12.2	10.6
Austria	25.7	35.3	23.0
Belgium	14.0	15.8	14.6
Denmark	18.6	16.8	20.3
Finland	9.6	16.8	20.4
France	22.2	19.1	15.9
Germany, West	21.9	25.9	18.8
Ireland	3.2	3.3	3.0
Italy	8.5	9.6	6.3
Japan	19.0	20.6	21.3
Netherlands	6.2	7.1	6.6
New Zealand	12.1	13.9	9.7
Norway	6.0	6.5	6.4
South Africa	10.5	11.2	12.2
Spain	5.1	4.7	5.2
Sweden	17.6	14.5	17.4
Switzerland	23.7	25.3	19.0
UK: England & Wales	9.9	12.3	11.2
Scotland	5.7	9.8	7.8
USA #	15.4	15.0	10.6

The number of USA states reporting suicides changed during these periods.

Dublin (1963) published suicide rates for twenty nations of the world for 1910-1914, 1926-1930, and 1960 (see Table 2.9). This permits us to calculate correlations for time periods of roughly 48 years and 32 years respectively. The Pearson product-moment correlations were 0.85 and 0.87 respectively, indicating a much greater consistency than for the one hundred year period.

These results, therefore, support the notion that national suicide rates are quite stable over time and thus meaningful for research study.

CONCLUSIONS

It can be seen that the majority of the studies reported in this chapter support the assumption that the official suicide and homicide rates as reported by the World Health Organization are reasonably valid. Differences in the suicide rates between countries are mirrored by their immigrant groups to the USA and to Australia. Changes in the classification of death codes did not have a significant impact on the relative rates of suicide or homicide. Finally, the suicide rates of the larger countries do remain quite stable over several decades. Thus we can conclude that the studies undertaken later in this book are based upon reasonably reliable and valid rates of suicide and homicide.

REFERENCES

Brooke, E. *Suicide and attempted suicide.* Geneva, Switzerland: World Health Organization, 1974.

Burvill, P., McCall, M., Stenhouse, N., & Reid, T. Deaths from suicide, motor vehicle accidents and all forms of violent deaths among migrants in Australia. *Acta Psychiatrica Scandinavica,* 1973, 49, 28-50.

Chia, B. H., & Tsoi, W. F. Suicide in Singapore. *Singapore Medical Journal,* 1972, 13, 91-97.

Douglas, J. D. *The social meanings of suicide.* Princeton, NJ: Princeton University Press, 1967.

Dublin, L. I. *Suicide.* New York: Ronald, 1963.

Durkheim, E. *Le Suicide.* Paris: Felix Alcan, 1897.

Interpol. *International Crime Statistics, 1979-1980.* Saint-Cloud, France: Interpol, undated.

Kalish, R. A. Suicide. *Bulletin of Suicidology,* 1968, December, 37-43.

Kramer, M., Pollack, E., Redick, R., & Locke, B. *Mental disorders/suicide.* Cambridge: Harvard University Press, 1972.

Lester, D. The validity of national suicide rates. *British Journal of Psychiatry,* 1980, 136, 107-108.

Lester, D. Coroners' decisions and suicide rates. *Psychological Reports* 1986, 58, 586.

Lester, D. The stability of national suicide rates. *Sociology & Social Research,* 1987, 71, 208.

Lester, D. Suicide in Zimbabwe. *Central African Journal of Medicine,* 1988, 34, 147-149.

Lester, D. Personal violence (suicide and homicide) in South Africa. *Acta Psychiatrica Scandinavica,* 1989a, 79, 235-237.

Lester, D. Suicide rates in immigrant groups and their countries of origin. *Psychological Reports,* 1989b, 65, 818.

Miller, L. Some data on suicide and attempted suicide of the Jewish population in Israel. *Mental Health & Society,* 1976, 3, 178-181.

Morselli, H. *Suicide.* New York: Appleton, 1882.

Rwegellera, G. Suicide rates in Lusaka, Zambia. *Psychological Medicine,* 1978, 8, 423-432.

Sainsbury, P., & Barraclough, B. M. Differences between suicide rates. *Science,* 1968, 220, 1252.

Smith, J. C., Mercy, J. A., & Rosenberg, M. L. Suicide and homicide among Hispanics in the Southwest. *Public Health Reports,* 1986, 101, 265-270.

Tan, C. T. Suicide trends in Singapore, 1975-1984. *Medicine, Science & the Law,* 1986, 26, 238-242.

Whitlock, F. Migration and suicide. *Medical Journal of Australia,* 1971, 2, 840-848.

World Health Organization. *World Health Statistics Annual, 1962.* Geneva, Switzerland: World Health Organization, 1965.

World Health Organization. *World Health Statistics Annual, 1971.* Geneva, Switzerland: World Health Organization, 1974.

World Health Organization. *World Health Statistics Annual.* Geneva, Switzerland: World Health Organization, 1977-1980.

CHAPTER 3

THE COLLECTION OF THE SUICIDE AND HOMICIDE RATES OF NATIONS OF THE WORLD

The basic source for the rates of suicide and homicide in nations of the world was the annual volume published by the World Health Organization, *World Health Statistics Annual*. The years chosen were 1969-1971 and 1979-1981. A three-year poeriod was chosen since data are often missing for one year in these volumes. The average of available data for each three-year period was calculated. These data were supplemented by the *Demographic Yearbook*, an annual publication from the United Nations.

To check on the comparability of World Health Organization and United Nations data, data from nations in 1980 with populations greater than one million was examined for both sets of data. The results are shown in Table 3.1. It can be seen that the rates are almost identical or within 0.1 for almost all of the suicide rates. Only Paraguay, Switzerland and Venezuela depart by more than this amount. For homicide, again all of the rates are identical or within 0.1 for almost all of the countries. Only Brazil, Guatemala, Paraguay and Venezuela depart from this, except for those countries still using the older classification system for diseases (identified in the *Demographic Yearbook* by BE codes). We may conclude that suicide rates are comparable for the two data sources, and that homicide rates are comparable if the later classification code is utilized (identified in the *Demographic Yearbook* as AM).

Table 3.1 A Comparison Of World Health Organization And United Nations Data For 1980

	Suicide Rates		Homicide Rates		
	UN	*WHO*	*UN*		*WHO*
			AM	*BE*	
Australia	10.9	11.0	1.9		1.9
Austria	25.6	25.7	1.2		1.2
Brazil	3.2	3.3	11.4		11.7
Bulgaria	13.6	13.6	2.5		2.5
Canada	14.0	14.0	2.1		2.1
Chile	4.9	4.9	2.6		2.6
Costa Rica	5.4	5.4	5.8		5.8
Denmark	31.6	31.6		5.7	1.3
Egypt	0.0	0.0	0.9		0.9
Finland	25.7	25.7		6.9	3.3
France	19.3	19.4	1.0		1.0
Germany, West	20.9	20.9	1.2		1.2
Greece	3.3	3.3	0.7		0.7
Guatemala	1.3	1.2	66.1		63.0
Hong Kong	13.6	13.5	1.6		1.6
Hungary	44.9	44.9	2.6		2.6
Ireland	6.3	6.3	0.7		0.7
Israel	6.0	6.0	1.8		1.8
Italy	7.4	7.3	1.9		1.9
Japan	17.6	17.6	1.0		1.0
Kuwait	0.7	0.7	0.9		0.9
Netherlands	10.1	10.1	0.8		0.8
New Zealand	10.8	10.8	1.3		1.3
Norway	12.4	12.4		2.0	1.1
Panama	2.0	2.1	2.1		2.2
Paraguay	1.7	3.1	5.0		9.1
Portugal	7.4	7.4	1.3		1.3

Table 3.1 (Continued)

Puerto Rico	9.1	9.1	15.1		15.1
Singapore	11.2	11.2	2.3		2.3
Spain	4.4	4.4	1.0		1.0
Sweden	19.4	19.4		8.8	1.2
Switzerland	25.4	25.7		2.0	1.0
UK: England &					
Wales	8.7	8.8	0.8		0.8
Northern Ireland	5.2	5.2	4.2		4.2
Scotland	10.0	10.0	1.6		1.6
USA	11.8	11.8	10.5		10.5
Venezuela	4.8	5.2	11.7		12.7
Yugoslavia	14.7	14.7	1.7		1.7

A search was made of the scholarly literature for articles which cited suicide or homicide rates. In addition, letters were sent to every foreign embassy in the USA requesting information. Occasional embassies sent data while most referred me to particular offices in their home nation. All referrals were contacted.

I contacted those who requested reprints of my research who were from nations which did not provide any data from these sources, and to members of the International Association for Suicide Prevention from nations for whom no data were yet available.

Data from all sources were compiled, and the results of this effort are shown in Tables 3.2 and 3.3.

TABLE 3.2

Suicide And Homicide Rates In 1969-1971

	Suicide			Homicide				
	total	male	female	total	male	female	years*	source
Argentina	10.0	15.3	4.8	7.3	12.2	2.4	2	WHO
Australia	12.7	17.1	8.2	1.5	1.9	1.2	3	
Austria	23.1	32.8	14.4	1.3	1.6	1.1	3	
Barbados	1.9	3.2	0.8	2.0	4.1	0.2	3	
Belgium	15.7	21.6	10.1	1.0	1.0	0.9	3	
Bulgaria	11.8	16.2	7.6	2.6	3.9	1.3	3	
Canada	11.4	16.3	6.3	2.0	2.6	1.4	3	
Chile	6.2	10.0	2.5	3.9	7.1	0.9	3	
Colombia	2.7	4.2	1.3	14.1	25.8	2.8	2	
Costa Rica	2.8	5.1	0.6	3.9	6.1	1.6	3/2	
Cuba	13.4	16.1	10.6	4.5	6.5	2.4	1	
Czechoslovakia	24.2	36.0	13.0	1.4	1.7	1.1	3	
Denmark	22.4	28.5	16.3	0.8	0.8	0.7	3	
Dominican Republic	2.5	3.5	1.9	4.9	8.4	1.4	3/2	
Ecuador	2.3	3.3	1.3	7.2	13.1	1.4	3/1	
El Salvador	7.6	13.2	2.1	19.5	55.5	3.9	3/2	
Finland	22.1	35.6	9.5	2.4	3.6	1.4	3	
France	15.5	22.9	8.5	0.8	1.0	0.6	3	
Germany, East	30.5	40.4	22.0	-	-	-	1	
Germany, West	21.0	27.8	14.9	1.3	1.6	1.0	3	
Greece	3.3	4.7	2.0	0.6	0.9	0.4	3	
Guatemala	3.2	4.9	1.4	20.2	36.7	3.6	3/2	
Hong Kong	10.6	11.7	9.4	1.5	2.3	0.6	3	
Hungary	34.7	50.4	19.9	2.1	2.7	1.5	3	
Iceland	7.5	11.1	4.0	0.5	0.5	0.5	2	
Ireland	2.1	3.2	1.0	0.4	0.5	0.2	3	
Israel	6.6	7.5	5.6	6.2	11.4	0.9	3	
Italy	5.7	8.0	3.5	0.9	1.2	0.5	3	
Japan	15.1	17.1	13.1	1.3	1.8	0.9	3	
Jordan	0.0	0.0	0.0	-	-	-	2	

Table 3.2 continued

Luxembourg	14.6	22.1	7.1	1.3	1.4	0.4	3
Malta	0.8	1.7	0.0	0.0	0.0	0.0	3
Mauritius	2.3	3.6	1.0	2.3	3.8	0.8	3
Mexico	0.8	1.4	0.3	14.1	25.9	2.3	3
Netherlands	7.9	9.6	6.2	0.5	0.7	0.4	3
New Zealand	9.3	12.0	6.6	1.1	1.3	0.9	3
Nicaragua	1.4	1.9	0.9	-	-	-	1
Norway	8.2	12.4	4.1	0.6	0.9	0.4	3
Panama	3.2	5.4	0.9	3.5	5.3	1.7	3/2
Paraguay	1.5	1.9	1.1	6.6	12.0	1.4	3/1
Peru	1.9	2.8	1.0	1.7	2.7	0.8	3/2
Philippines	0.7	0.8	0.6	11.9	22.5	1.4	3
Poland	11.4	19.0	4.1	1.1	1.4	0.7	3
Portugal	8.0	12.9	3.4	0.9	1.2	0.6	3
Puerto Rico	9.7	14.6	5.1	12.4	21.1	4.1	3/1
Singapore	9.7	11.3	8.0	1.8	2.9	0.6	3
Monaco	37.5			-			2
Montserrat	3.3			-			1
Mozambique	0.8	1.1	0.3	-			2/1/1
Pacific Is.	7.0			-			3
Panama	3.3			-			3
Paraguay	1.5			-			2
Portugese Timor	0.1			-			2
Puerto Rico	9.5			-			2
Reunion	6.9			-			1
Ryuku Is.	11.9			-			3
St Kitts/Nevis/ Lucia/Anguila	0.5			-			3
San Marino	16.7			-			3
Sao Tome & Principe	2.4			-			3
Seychelles	2.0			-			2
Syria	0.2			-			3
Trinidad & Tobago	6.6			-			3
Uruguay	10.3			-			3
Wallis & Futuna Is.	0.0			-			1
Western Samoa	3.2			-			2
Yugoslavia	13.7			-			3

Table 3.2 continued

India	8.1			-			1	Headley
Jamaica	1.4	2.7	0.2	-			2	Burke
Jordan	1.4			-			1	Headley
Fiji	8.4	8.7	8.2	-			2	Price & Karim$
India	8.2			-			3	Rao
India	8.4			2.9			3	Krishna
Lithuania	24.3			-			3	pc+
Sri Lanka	19.0	25.1	10.9	-			3	Headley
Syria	1.5			-			3	Headley
Taiwan	12.1			-			3	Headley
Zimbabwe	6.0	9.5	2.4	-			1	Rittey & Castle
Tokelau	0.0			0.0			1	
UK Virgin Islands	0.0			0.0			1	
Fiji *	25.2	28.3	22.0	-			1	Haynes
Greenland	80.3			-			3	Thorslund et
Jordan	2.8			-			3	Headley
Jordan	1.7			2.4			3	Daradkeh/pc
Korea	20.6			-			1	Huk
South Africa	5.3	8.4	2.2	22.5	38.1	6.3	3	Lester
Taiwan	9.9	11.1	8.6	-			2	Headley
Teneriffe	8.9	13.9	4.0	-			3	Marco et
US Virgin Islands	2.4	3.6	1.3	19.7	33.9	6.6	3	US Vital Statistics
Germany, East	-			0.9			3	pc
Greenland	54.9	84.2	20.4	-			3	pc
India	6.0	6.9	5.1	3.2			3	pc
Lithuania	34.1			-			3	pc
Malaysia	0.6			-			1	pc
Saudi Arabia	1.3			1.3			3	pc
Trinidad & Tobago	4.8	7.0	2.6	3.3	4.3	2.4	3	pc
Turkey	1.8			-			3	pc
Zimbabwe	6.1	9.9	2.6	16.7	29.2	5.4	2	pc

* years of data for suicide and homicide rates are separated by a "/"
# rates from the Demographic Yearbook and other sources were used to supplement WHO rates
+ personal communication
$ 1971-1972
* 1981-1982
# includes suicide and attempted suicide

Table 3.3

Suicide And Homicide Rates In Nations Of The World In 1979-1981

	Suicide			Homicide				
	total	male	female	total	male	female	years	source
Argentina	7.2	9.7	4.3	3.7	5.3	1.9	2	WHO
Australia	11.3	16.6	5.9	1.9	2.4	1.3	3	
Austria	26.0	38.3	14.9	1.3	1.3	1.2	3	
Bahamas	0.5	1.0	0.0	10.2	16.8	3.7	2	
Barbados	1.5	2.6	0.5	4.2	6.9	1.5	3	
Belgium	21.5	28.2	15.0	1.6	1.8	1.4	1	
Belize	0.6	1.3	0.0	0.0	0.0	0.0	1	
Brazil	3.4	4.7	2.1	11.5	20.8	2.3	2	
Bulgaria	13.9	19.4	8.3	2.7	4.2	1.3	3	
Canada	14.1	21.3	6.9	2.3	3.0	1.6	3	
Cape Verde	2.4	4.4	0.6	1.0	1.5	0.6	1	
Cayman Islands	6.0	12.3	0.0	0.0	0.0	0.0	1	
Chile	5.5	9.3	1.8	2.7	4.5	0.9	3	
Costa Rica	4.4	7.0	1.7	4.7	7.6	1.9	3	
Czechoslovakia	19.8	30.3	9.9	1.1	1.2	1.0	1	
Denmark	29.1	37.3	21.1	1.2	1.2	1.3	3	
Dominica	0.0	0.0	0.0	4.8	9.7	0.0	1	
Ecuador	2.8	3.5	2.1	6.0	10.5	1.4	1	
Egypt	0.1	0.1	0.05	0.8	1.3	0.3	2	
El Salvador	9.7	14.7	4.6	37.6	67.6	7.4	1	
Finland	24.7	40.4	10.0	2.9	4.3	1.5	3	
France	19.2	27.9	10.9	1.0	1.3	0.8	3	
Germany, West	21.4	29.0	14.4	1.2	1.3	1.0	3	
Greece	3.2	4.4	2.0	0.7	1.1	0.4	3	
Guatemala	1.0	1.8	0.2	64.4	118.8	10.9	3	
Hong Kong	12.4	13.5	11.1	1.5	2.2	0.8	3	
Hungary	45.0	63.9	27.3	2.5	3.0	1.9	3	
Iceland	10.2	15.1	5.3	1.3	2.0	0.6	3	
Ireland	6.2	8.7	3.7	1.2	1.6	0.8	3	
Israel	6.0	7.8	4.1	1.8	2.5	1.1	3	
Italy	7.1	9.9	4.3	1.8	3.0	0.7	3	
Japan	17.5	22.2	13.0	1.0	1.1	0.8	3	
Jordan	0.0	0.0	0.0	-	-	-	1	
Kuwait	0.7	0.9	0.5	0.9	1.0	0.7	1	
Luxembourg	16.5	23.4	10.0	1.8	1.1	2.4	2	
Malta	0.0	0.0	0.0	1.9	2.6	1.2	1	
Martinique	11.9	20.0	4.4	1.0	0.7	1.3	1	
Mauritius	3.9	5.8	2.1	1.6	2.6	0.6	3	
Mexico	1.7	2.6	0.7	17.5	31.9	3.0	1	
Montserrat	0.0	0.0	0.0	0.0	0.0	0.0	1	
Netherlands	10.2	12.3	8.1	0.8	1.1	0.5	3	
Netherland Antilles	2.0	3.2	0.8	1.6	3.2	0.0	1	
New Zealand	10.2	14.5	5.9	1.4	1.6	1.1	3	
Norway	12.4	18.2	6.7	1.1	1.5	0.8	3	
Panama	2.0	3.3	0.6	2.3	3.8	0.7	2	
Papua-New Guinea	0.2	0.1	0.2	0.1	0.2	0.1	1	

Table 3.3 continued

Paraguay	2.7	3.0	2.4	9.5	17.2	1.9	2
Poland	12.7	21.8	4.0	1.0	1.3	0.7	1
Portugal	8.3	12.5	4.5	1.4	2.1	0.6	3
Puerto Rico	8.5	14.6	2.7	14.6	26.9	2.8	2
St Kitts & Nevis	0.8	1.7	0.0	0.0	0.0	0.0	3
St Lucia	0.8	1.7	0.0	0.8	0.8	0.8	2
St Vincent Grenadines	0.9	1.9	0.0	1.8	1.9	1.7	1
Seychelles	3.1	3.1	3.1	0.0	0.0	0.0	1
Singapore	9.8	10.8	8.9	1.9	2.7	1.1	3
Spain	4.4	6.6	2.2	1.0	1.6	0.4	3
Sri Lanka	29.0	37.7	19.7	2.3	3.9	0.6	1
Suriname	14.2	17.8	10.8	4.4	6.3	2.5	3
Sweden	19.1	26.8	11.6	1.3	1.6	1.0	3
Switzerland	24.7	34.9	15.0	1.0	0.9	1.1	3
Syria	0.4	0.6	0.1	0.05	0.05	0.0	2
Thailand	7.1	7.4	6.9	25.8	45.8	5.4	3
Trinidad & Tobago	5.2	7.4	2.9	3.0	3.9	2.0	1
Turkey	0.2	0.3	0.2	-	-	-	1
UK: England & Wales	8.7	11.0	6.6	0.8	0.8	0.7	3
Northern Ireland	5.0	7.1	3.1	4.2	7.6	0.9	2
Scotland	9.9	12.7	7.1	1.6	2.2	1.0	3
USA	12.0	18.6	5.7	10.2	16.4	4.4	3
Venezuela	4.7	7.6	1.9	11.2	20.6	1.7	2
Yugoslavia	14.8	21.0	8.8	2.1	2.9	1.2	3
							Demographic Yearbook
Antigua	1.0			-			1
Bermuda	2.8			3.7			2
British Virgin Is	0.0			0.0			1
Colombia	3.5			37.4			1
Cook Islands	0.0			0.0			1
Dominican Republic	2.0			-			1
El Salvador	12.1			88.6			3/2
Faeroe Islands	6.9			-			2
Falkland Islands	0.0			33.3			3
Fiji	15.1			5.8			3
Gibralta	0.0			0.0			3
Greenland	66.2	70.8	20.7	-			3/1/1
Guadeloupe	9.5			0.9			1
Guam	6.8			12.4			3/2
Honduras	1.2	2.1	0.4	9.5	17.2	1.7	1
Isle of Man	11.6			0.0			3
Liechtenstein	9.0			-			3
Macao	0.0			-			1
Monaco	0.0			0.0			2/1
Niue	0.0			25.0			1
Paraguay	1.5			5.4			3
Peru	1.2			1.0			1
Philippines	8.3			-			1
St Helena	18.2			-			2
Samoa	1.3			0.0			1
San Marino	6.2			-			3
Seychelles	3.2			0.0			3/1
Sri Lanka	27.8			2.6			3/2

Table 3.3 continued

Spain	4.3	6.6	2.1	0.3	0.5	0.2	3
Sweden	21.5	30.3	12.7	0.9	1.1	0.7	3
Switzerland	18.2	26.3	10.4	0.6	0.7	0.6	3
Taiwan	13.2	15.6	10.5	1.2	1.8	0.6	1
Thailand	3.9	4.4	3.3	17.1	30.5	3.7	3
Trinidad & Tobago	5.2	8.3	2.0	3.9	5.3	2.4	2
UK: England & Wales	8.3	9.9	6.8	0.7	0.8	0.7	3
Northern Ireland	4.5	5.5	3.5	1.0	1.7	0.3	3
Scotland	7.3	9.0	5.7	1.2	1.7	0.9	3
USA	11.4	16.5	6.5	8.3	13.5	3.5	3
Uruguay	10.1	15.4	5.0	3.7	6.5	0.8	3/1
Venezuela	6.8	9.5	4.1	7.9	13.9	1.7	3
Yugoslavia	13.9	20.3	7.6	3.4	5.3	1.6	1
							Demographic Yearbook#
American Samoa	6.7			-			2
Angola	1.0			-			3
Bahamas	0.0			-			2
Belize	0.8			-			2
Bermuda	6.0			-			2
British Virgin Is.	26.7			-			3
Canal Zone	6.7			-			2
Cape Verde Is.	3.7			-			3
Cayman Is.	10.0			-			2
Channel Is.	8.8			-			2
Cook Is.	0.2			-			3
Costa Rica	2.9			-			3
Cuba	12.7	13.8	10.0	-			3/1/1
Dominican Republic	2.5			-			3
Ecuador	2.3			-			3
Egypt	0.0			-			2
El Salvador	7.9			-			3
Faeroe Is.	2.5			-			3
Falkland Is.	0.0			-			1
Fiji	1.5	6.3	1.5	-			3/1/1
French Guiana	6.0	3.7	8.7	-			1
French Polynesia	0.8			-			1
Germany, East	29.6			-			2
Gibralta	3.3			-			3
Greenland	8.7			-			3
Grenada	1.0			-			1
Guadeloupe	3.4			-			1
Guam	5.7			-			3
Guatemala	3.2			-			3
Guinea-Bissau	12.7	19.4	6.4	-			1
Iceland	9.5			-			3
Iraq	0.0			-			1
Isle of Man	9.4			-			3
Jamaica	1.2			-			3
Jordan	0.1			-			3
Kenya	0.2	0.2	0.2	-			1
Kuwait	0.3			-			2
Leichtenstein	5.0			-			1
Macao	7.7	6.3	9.1	-			2/1/1
Martinique	5.4						1

REFERENCES

Burke, A. W. Suicide in Jamaica. *West Indian Medical Journal*, 1985, 34(1), 48-52.

Daradkeh, T. K. The possible reasons behind a high intentional homicide rate in Jordan. *Dirasat*, 1988, 15(4), 59-69.

Haynes, R. Suicide in Fiji. *British Journal of Psychiatry*, 1984, 145, 433-438.

Headley, L. A. *Suicide in Asia and the Near East*. Berkeley: University of California, 1983.

Huk, J. H. Suicide by burning. In R. I. Yufit (Ed.) *Proceedings of the 20th Annual Conference*. Denver: American Association of Suicidology, 1988, 189-190.

Krishna, K. P. Suicide and homicide in India. *Indian Journal of Criminology & Criminalistics*, 1981, 1(1), 107-108.

Lester, D. Personal violence (suicide and homicide) in South Africa. *Acta Psychiatrica Scandinavica*, 1989, 79, 235-237.

Lester, D., & Wilson, C. Suicide in Zimbabwe. *Central African Journal of Medicine*, 1988, 34, 147-149.

Marco, G. R., Pulido, R. F., Funero, M. A., Doresto, J., & de Rivera, G. J. L. Suicide on Teneriffe Island. *European Journal of Psychiatry*, 1988, 2, 1170-188.

Price, J., & Karim, J. Suicide in Fiji. *Acta Psychiatrica Scandinavica*, 1975, 52, 153-159.

Rao, V. Adolescent suicide behaviour in India. In A. Aalberg (ed.) *Proceedings of the 9th International Congress for Suicide Prevention and Crisis Intervention*. Helsinki: Finnish Association for Mental Health, 1978, 133-138.

Rittey, D. A. W., & Castle, W. M. Suicides in Rhodesia. *Central African Journal of Medicine*, 1972, 18, 97-100.

Thorslund, J., & Misfeldt, J. On suicide statistics. *Arctic Medical Researech*, 1989, 48, 124-130.

CHAPTER 4

THE CHOICE OF THE SAMPLE

For the basic sample to be used for the research in this book, nations were chosen whose 1980 population was greater than one million, since this ensures reasonably reliable suicide rates. Table 4.1 lists those nations of the world meeting this criterion together with their population and gross domestic product per capita obtained from Summers and Heston (1984).

The suicide and homicide rates where available are also listed in Table 4.1 and derived from the rates reported in Chapter 3. Sometimes, the rates for different sources were averaged, but preference was also given to those sources with more years of data available.

Bias in the Choice of Sample

It can be seen that the majority of African nations do not have suicide and homicide rates available for use. These nations, therefore will be under-represented in the sample. In contrast, almost all European nations do have rates available, and so they will be over-represented.

This raises the issue of the importance of the sample in determining the results of cross-national analyses of social indicators, an issue not previous studied in cross-national studies of suicide except by Lester and Stack (1989). The present study took three social indicators and explored

Table 4.1

The Set Of Suicide And Homicide Rates For 1970 And 1980

	gross domestic product/capita 1980	population in thousands 1980	suicide rate 1970	suicide rate 1980	homicide rate 1970	homicide rate 1980
Africa						
Algeria	2043	18669				
Angola	781	7723*	1.0	-	-	-
Benin	415	3464				
Burkina Faso	277	6962				
Burundi	379	4114				
Cameroon	940	8701				
Central Africa	490	2320				
Chad	338	4477				
Congo Peopl R	1067	1630				
Egypt	1177	40792	0.0	0.1	-	0.8
Ethiopia	337	37717				
Ghana	739	10740				
Guinea	711	5407*				
Ivory Coast	1410	8194				
Kenya	460	16632	0.2	-	-	-
Lesotho	605	1355				
Liberia	828	1879				
Libya	-	3043				
Madagascar	549	8714				
Malawi	344	6091				
Mali	250	6590				
Mauritania	682	1551				
Morocco	1261	19382				
Mozambique	705	12103	0.8	-	-	-
Niger	563	5515				
Nigeria	1476	84732				
Rwanda	419	5139				
Senegal	690	5538				
Sierra Leone	526	3255				
Somalia	422	4674				
South Africa	2354	28270	-	5.3	-	22.5
Sudan	860	18681				
Tanzania	492	18757				
Togo	675	2578				
Tunisia	1857	6384				
Uganda	535	12637				
Zaire	296	26225				
Zambia	672	5647				
Zimbabwe	930	7009	6.0	6.1	-	16.7
Asia						
Afghanistan	306	15951*				
Bangladesh	432	88000				
Bhutan	-	1165				
Burma	359	33637*				
China	1135	981000				

Table 4.1 continued

Hong Kong	3973	5039	10.6	12.4	1.5	1.5
India	498	687000	8.3	6.0	2.9	3.2
Indonesia	734	148000				
Iran	1796	38345				
Iraq	2783	13238*	0.0	-	-	-
Israel	4041	3878	6.6	6.0	6.2	1.8
Japan	5996	117000	15.1	17.5	1.3	1.0
Jordan	1064	1923	0.7	2.2	-	2.4
Korea Rep	2007	38124	-	20.6	-	-
Kuwait	-	1375	0.3	0.7	-	0.9
Malaysia	2204	13764	-	0.6	-	-
Nepal	405	14640				
Pakistan	663	82581				
Philippines	1022	49253	0.7	-	11.9	-
Saudi Arabia	-	9732	-	1.3	-	1.3
Singapore	3948	2415	9.7	9.8	1.8	1.9
Sri Lanka	838	14738	19.0	27.8	-	2.6
Syria	2199	8800	0.6	0.4	-	0.05
Taiwan	2522	17805#	12.1	9.9	1.2	-
Thailand	1181	46700	3.9	7.1	17.1	25.8
United Arab E	-	1015				
<u>N & Cent. America</u>						
Canada	7521	24043	11.4	14.1	2.0	2.3
Costa Rica	2170	2218	2.8	4.4	3.9	4.7
Cuba	-	9724*	12.7	-	4.5	
Dominican Rep.	1564	5697	2.5	2.0	4.9	-
El Salvador	899	4525	7.7	12.1	19.5	88.6
Guatemala	1422	6916	3.2	1.0	20.2	64.4
Haiti	439	5413				
Honduras	1031	3662	-	1.2	-	9.5
Jamaica	1414	2133	1.3	-	-	-
Mexico	2547	70416	0.8	1.7	14.1	17.5
Nicaragua	1324	2771	1.4	-	-	-
Panama	2157	1956	3.2	2.0	3.5	2.3
Puerto Rico	-	3206*	9.7	8.5	12.4	14.6
Trinidad & T	3994	1082	6.6	4.8	3.9	3.3
USA	8089	228000	11.4	12.0	8.3	10.2
<u>South America</u>						
Argentina	3209	28237	10.0	7.2	7.3	3.7
Bolivia	1114	5570				
Brazil	2152	121000	-	3.4	-	11.5
Chile	2372	11145	6.2	5.5	3.9	2.7
Colombia	1882	26906	2.7	3.5	14.1	37.4
Ecuador	1556	8123	2.3	2.8	7.2	6.0
Paraguay	1753	3147	1.5	1.5	6.6	5.4
Peru	1810	17295	1.9	1.2	1.7	1.0
Uruguay	3269	2914	10.2	-	3.7	-
Venezuela	3310	15024	6.8	4.7	7.9	11.2
<u>Australasia</u>						
Australia	6308	14692	12.7	11.3	1.5	1.9
New Zealand	4553	3113	9.3	10.2	1.1	1.4

Table 4.1 continued

Papua N Guin	996	3070	-	0.2	-	0.1
<u>Europe</u>						
Austria	6052	7554	23.1	26.0	1.3	1.3
Belgium	6293	9847	15.7	21.5	1.0	1.6
Bulgaria	3437	8862	11.2	13.9	2.6	2.7
Czechoslovakia	4908	15311*	24.2	19.8	1.4	1.1
Denmark	6746	5123	22.4	29.1	0.8	1.2
Finland	5939	4780	22.1	24.7	2.4	2.9
France	6678	53880	15.5	19.2	0.8	1.0
Germany East	5532	16737*	29.6	-	-	0.9
Germany West	6967	61566	21.0	21.4	1.3	1.2
Greece	3946	9643	3.3	3.2	0.6	0.7
Hungary	3861	10710	34.7	45.0	2.1	2.5
Ireland	3467	3401	2.1	6.2	0.4	1.2
Italy	4661	56434	5.7	7.1	0.9	1.8
Netherlands	5856	14150	7.9	10.2	0.5	0.8
Norway	6825	4091	8.2	12.4	0.6	1.1
Poland	3509	35578	11.4	12.7	1.1	1.0
Portugal	3092	9766	8.0	8.3	0.9	1.4
Romania	2766	22201*				
Spain	4264	37386	4.3	4.4	0.3	1.0
Sweden	7143	8310	21.5	19.1	0.9	1.3
Switzerland	6610	6385	18.2	24.7	0.6	1.0
Turkey	2069	44823	-	1.8	-	-
UK	4990	56330	8.1	8.6	0.8	1.0
England & Wales			8.3	8.7	0.7	0.8
Northern Ireland			4.5	5.0	1.0	4.2
Scotland			7.3	9.9	1.2	1.6
USSR	3943	265542*				
Yugoslavia	2593	22304	13.7	14.8	3.4	2.1

Note: All populations come from World Bank (1991) except for those marked with an * which come from United Nations (1989).
 # personal communication from Academia Sinica, Taiwan

their associations in samples of nations chosen on different bases. The three social indicators chosen were based on previous research findings: the quality of life, the gross domestic product per capita, and the suicide rate. Lester (1984) has shown that suicide rates were positively related to both the gross national product per capita and the quality of life.

For the year 1970, ratings of the gross domestic product per capita for each nation of the world were obtained from Summers and Heston (1984). Ratings of the quality of life (for 1969) were obtained from Estes (1984). The data set is shown in Table 4.2

Table 4.2 The Set Of 1970 Suicide Rates For The Biased Sample Analyses

	gross domestic product/capita 1970	**suicide rate 1970**	**quality of life 1969**
Africa			
**Angola*	1333	1.0	-
**Egypt*	755	0.0	72
**Kenya*	431	0.2	68
**Mozambique*	1007	0.8	-
**Zimbabwe*	958	6.0	80
Asia			
Hong Kong	2005	10.6	-
India	450	8.3	46
Iraq	1602	0.0	64
**Israel*	3419	6.6	87
**Japan*	4215	15.1	149
Jordan	935	0.7	42
Kuwait	-	0.3	-
Philippines	781	0.7	98
**Singapore*	2012	9.7	106
Sri Lanka	765	19.0	119
Syria	1041	0.6	71
Taiwan	1298	12.1	-
Thailand	791	3.9	104

Table 4.2 (Continued)

N S & Cent America			
Argentina	2750	10.0	116
Canada	5703	11.4	157
**Chile*	2090	6.2	135
Colombia	1355	2.7	117
Costa Rica	1601	2.8	138
Cuba	-	12.7	140
Dominican Rep	1113	2.5	113
Ecuador	954	2.3	108
El Salvador	902	7.7	115
Guatemala	1133	3.2	66
Jamaica	1841	1.3	130
Mexico	2005	0.8	120
Nicaragua	1246	1.4	83
Panama	1804	3.2	128
Paraguay	1004	1.5	115
Peru	1626	1.9	82
Puerto Rico	-	9.7	-
**Trinidad & T*	1847	6.6	123
USA	6629	11.4	91
Uruguay	2648	10.2	137
**Venezuela*	3667	6.8	128
Europe & Australasia			
**Australia*	5552	12.7	173
**Austria*	4154	23.1	186
Belgium	4771	15.7	175
Bulgaria	2738	11.2	167
Czechoslovakia	4027	24.2	151
Denmark	5530	22.4	198
Finland	4549	22.1	169
France	5041	15.5	172
Germany E	4100	29.6	-
Germany W	5356	21.0	179
Greece	2672	3.3	136
Hungary	3077	34.7	173
Ireland	2717	2.1	185

Table 4.2 (Continued)

Italy	3655	5.7	160
Netherlands	4767	7.9	187
New Zealand	4137	9.3	178
**Norway*	4511	8.2	186
Poland	2731	11.4	168
Portugal	2126	8.0	131
Spain	3231	4.3	156
Sweden	6025	21.5	198
Switzerland	5858	18.2	164
UK	4216	8.1	171
Yugoslavia	2027	13.7	140

* nations used in the representative sample

Three samples of nations were used: (1) the total available sample, (2) a sample of eighteen industrialized nations used by Lynn (1971), and (3) a representative sample of nations. To arrive at this latter sample, since suicide rates were available for five of the 39 African nations in 1970 (that is 12.8%), the same rough proportion of nations was chosen for Asia (three out of 27), North, Central and South America (three out of 25) and Europe and Australasia (three out of 28). The nations chosen for Asia, America and Europe/Australasia were chosen by using a table of random numbers and indicated by asterisks in Table 4.2.

The results are shown in Table 4.3. It can be seen that the correlations for both the total sample and for the representative sample indicate strong associations between the suicide rate and both the quality of life and the gross national product per capita.

In contrast, the correlations were much lower for the sample of industrialized nations, and two failed to reach significance. It can be seen that the sample of industrialized nations was characterized by higher ratings for the quality of life, higher gross domestic products per capita, and higher suicide rates.

A representative sample of nations of the world is the preferable methodology if an investigator is interested in studying the *world* and if not all nations report suicide rates. Samples of all reporting nations typically include an over-representation of industrialized nations and an underrepresentation of under-developed nations. In particular, data are hard to find for Africa, North Africa and the Indian Continent. However, it is interesting to note that in the present study, the results from the total available sample were similar to those obtained from an effort to choose a more representative sample.

Table 4.3 Correlations Between The Social Indicators For Different Samples Of Nations, 1970

sample	quality of life & suicide	quality of life & gdp/capita	gdp/capita & suicide	
total	0.62***	0.73***	0.62***	61
representative	0.77***	0.86***	0.77***	14
Lynn	0.19	- 0.33	0.48*	18

means and (standard deviations)

	suicide rate	quality of life	gdp/capita
total	9.1 (8.0)	131 (41)	2721 (1706)
representative	7.4 (6.4)	124 (43)	2594 (1677)
Lynn	14.0 (6.4)	171 (24)	4855 (956)

* one-tailed $p < 0.05$
** one-tailed $p < 0.01$
*** one-tailed $p < 0.001$

Thus, it appears reasonable to use the total available sample for studies of the world rather than attempting to choose a representative sample, especially since a truly representative sample is impossible without drastically reducing the sample size and, therefore, the reliability of the results.

References

Estes, R. J. *The social progress of nations*. New York: Praeger, 1984.

Lester, D. The association between the quality of life and suicide and homicide rates. *Journal of Social Psychology*, 1984, 124, 247-248.

Lester, D., & Stack, S. Bias resulting from the choice of sample and results of cross-national analyses of suicide rates. *Quality & Quantity*, 1989, 23, 221-223.

Lynn, R. *Personality and national character*. New York: Pergamon, 1971.

Summers, R., & Heston, A. Improved international comparisons of real product and its composition. *Review of Income & Wealth*, 1984, 30, 207-262.

United Nations. *Demographic Yearbook 1987*. New York: United Nations, 1989.

World Bank. *World Tables 1991*. Baltimore: Johns Hopkins University Press, 1991.

CHAPTER 5

A CORRELATIONAL ANALYSIS

A number of studies have appeared in the past examining which social variables are associated with national suicide and homicide rates. Based on these studies, a search was made of data sources in order to identify data on the social characteristics of nations in 1980 which might be useful in the present study.

THE SOCIAL VARIABLES USED

Several possible sources of data were identified, with some overlap in the variables measured. When there was duplication, both sets of values for a particular variable were included in the data set so that the reliability of the correlations could be examined.

The data sources and the social characteristics were for 1980 [except for those in items (11), (13) and (14)].

(1) gross domestic product and the population from Chapter 4 of the present book,

(2) the quality of life (Estes, 1984),

(3) the extent of civil liberties from Gastil (1980),

(4) an index of violations of the 'integrity of the person' from Lindgren (1990),

(5) the total fertility rate and infant mortality rates, life expectancy at birth, percentage of urban population, and percentage of females in the labor force from the World Bank (1991),

(6) the crude marriage, divorce and birth rates from the United Nations (1986, 1990),

(7) the population density, percentage of urban population, urban population growth rate, marriage rate, divorce rate, percentage of the population over 65 years of age, ratio of illegitimate/legitimate births, area of the country, birth rate 1975-1980, death rate 1975-1980, percentage of Christians, percentage of Muslims, gross national product growth rate 1970-1979, inflation rate 1970-1980, percentage of population aged 15-64 working (known as the employment ratio), percentage of women in the labor force, percentage of people under the age of 15 and over the age of 65 (known as the dependency ratio), unemployment rate, percentage of workers in unions, person-days lost in strikes per working population, number of industrial disputes per working population, percentage of children in the labor force, infant mortality (for infants aged 0-1), quality of life, population per hospital bed, population per doctor, calories consumed per capita, number of pharmacists per capita, number of soldiers per capita, defense expenditures as a percentage of the gross domestic product, defense expenditures per capita, and percentage of males in the total population from Kurian (1984)[5] ,

(8) the alcohol consumption per capita for 1977 from Adrian (1984),

(9) the consumption of corn per capita from the US Department of Agriculture (1983),

(10) literacy, population per nurse, growth rate in the gross national product 1970-1980, population growth 1970-1980, male labor force participation, and percentage of the population aged 0-14 from the World Bank (1983a, 1983b, 1983c),

(11) the average height and weight of 12 year olds from Eveleth and Tanner (1976) and the ectomorphy scores calculated by the present author (height divided by the cube root of the weight),

(12) political freedom, a freedom index, and literacy from Barrett (1982),

(13) indices of political rights and civil rights from Taylor and Jodice (1983), and

(14) the percentage of Christians, Roman Catholics and Muslims from Taylor and Hudson (1972).

---

5 In some of the tables prepared by Kurian, a single nation appears twice with two separate values for the variable. In such cases, that nation's data were not used.

The Correlations

The Pearson correlations between the suicide and homicide rates and the social variables are shown in Table 5.1. Suicide rates were associated with the gross domestic product per capita, quality of life, birth rates, infant mortality, life expectancy, male and female participation in the labor force, divorce rates (for one of the two measures), growth rate in the urban population, percentages of the elderly and children, illegitimate births, percentage of Muslims, unionization, strikes, hospital beds per capita, pharmacists per capita, caloric intake, percentage of men in the population, alcohol consumption, literacy, and growth in the total population.

The homicide rate was associated with gross domestic product per capita, quality of life, birth rates, infant mortality, life expectancy, percentage of the urban population, marriage rates, percentages of the elderly and children, illegitimate births, unionization, hospital beds per capita, doctors per capita, caloric intake, and alcohol consumption.

Let us look at how these associations mesh with theory.

Theories of Suicide

Durkheim

Durkheim (1897) argued that social suicide rates would be associated with two broad social characteristics: social integration (the degree to which people are bound together in social networks) and social regulation (the degree to which the behaviors, desires and emotions of the people are governed by social norms and customs). Durkheim saw the relationship as curvilinear, but sociologists today see the relationship as linear, at least for modern societies (Johnson, 1965).

Table 5.1 Pearson Correlations Between Suicide And Homicide Rates And Social Variables In Nations Of The World, 1980

	suicide		homicide	
	r	n	r	n
homicide rate#	-0.15	57	-	
gdp/capita	0.54***	59	-0.37**	55
population	0.05	62	-0.03	58
quality of life	0.54***	56	-0.33*	52
civil liberties	-0.15	60	0.18	56
violations of the person	-0.20	39	0.11	35
fertility	-0.63***	58	0.35**	54
infant mortality	-0.52***	58	0.36**	54
life expectancy	0.47***	58	-0.42***	54
% urban population	0.20	57	-0.29*	53
females in labor force	0.63***	56	-0.17	52
marriage rate	0.19	55	-0.25	53
divorce rate	0.33*	46	-0.21	44
birth rate	-0.54***	45	0.50***	45
population density	0.06	58	-0.07	56
% urban	0.19	60	-0.26*	57
urban population growth	-0.54***	60	0.17	57
marriage rate	0.27*	55	-0.37**	52
divorce rate	0.21	44	-0.15	43
% elderly	0.60***	61	-0.35**	57
illegitimate births	-0.45**	42	0.60***	42
area	0.14	61	0.01	57
birth rate	-0.66***	61	0.37**	58
death rate	-0.05	61	-0.16	58
% Christians	0.08	62	0.16	58
% Muslims	-0.33**	62	-0.14	58
gnp growth rate	0.03	61	-0.12	58
inflation rate	-0.15	54	-0.06	50
unemployment rate	0.05	50	-0.06	45
employment ratio	0.62***	62	-0.24	58
females in labor force	0.61***	60	-0.19	57
dependence ratio	-0.66***	60	0.41***	58
% workers in union	0.49***	50	-0.32*	46

Table 5.1 (Continued)

strike days/worker	0.07	41	-0.11	38
strikes/worker	0.29	40	-0.10	37
working children	-0.41**	52	0.27	48
infant mortality	-0.41**	59	0.25	56
quality of life	0.55***	62	-0.28*	58
hospital beds/capita	-0.36**	61	0 27*	58
doctors/capita	-0.25	59	0.27*	57
calories/capita	0.52***	58	-0.44***	55
pharmacists/capita	0.41**	49	-0.21	46
soldiers/capita	0.04	60	-0.24	56
% defense expenditures	-0.17	59	-0.14	55
defense expend/capita	0.04	59	-0.20	55
% males	-0.46***	60	0.02	56
male life expectancy	0.50***	60	-0.35**	57
alcohol consumption	0.52***	54	-0.31*	51
corn consumption	-0.06	57	0.10	53
literacy	0.59***	52	-0.17	48
nurses/capita	-0.37**	57	0.24	53
gnp growth rate	-0.01	57	-0.10	53
population growth rate	-0.66***	61	0.28*	58
males in labor force	0.52***	60	-0.27*	57
% under 15 years of age	-0.69***	60	0.39**	57
height	0.36*	40	-0.22	37
weight	0.28	37	-0.05	34
ectomorphy	0.07	37	-0.21	34
political freedom	-0.09	62	-0.11	58
freedom index	0.18	62	-0.08	58
literacy	0.58***	62	-0.25	58
political rights index	-0.14	59	0.07	55
civil rights index	-0.16	59	0.15	55
% Christians	0.12	61	0.12	57
% Roman Catholics	-0.15	61	0.27*	57
% Muslims	-0.30*	61	-0.12	57

the variables are in the order in which they are listed in the text

* two-tailed p < .05

** two-tailed p < .01

*** two-tailed p < .001

The presence of children and a high marriage rate should increase social integration and be associated with lower suicide rates, while a high divorce rate should weaken social integration and be associated with a higher suicide rate. This has been confirmed in studies of nations by Stack (1980, 1981). In the present analysis, suicide rates were negatively associated with birth rates and positively associated with divorce rates as predicted, but suicide rates were *positively* associated with marriage rates, opposite to the prediction. The reasons for this anomaly are far from clear at the present time.

Lester (1988) noted that strike action promotes social solidarity and, therefore, according to Durkheim's theory, should be associated with lower suicide rates. The present study, however, found the opposite association, that is, a *positive* association between suicide rates and both unionization (statistically significant) and strike actions (not statistically significant).

ECONOMIC DEVELOPMENT

Empirical research has shown that suicide rates are positively associated with economic development. Suicide rates are higher in nations with a higher level of economic development and quality of life (Conklin and Simpson, 1987; Haas, 1969; Lester, 1984). Lester interpreted this finding using Henry and Short's (1954) theory of suicide. Henry and Short argued that suicide rates would be high when there were no obvious external constraints on behavior and no external causes to blame for one's misery. Therefore, as the material conditions of life improve, there should be fewer obvious external sources of blame and, therefore, higher suicide rates.

The present results support this prediction. Suicide rates were positively associated with the quality of life, the gross domestic product per capita, life expectancy, caloric intake, literacy, and (negatively) with infant mortality.

OTHER VARIABLES

There has been a great deal of research linking unemployment with suicide (Platt, 1984). However, in the present analysis, unemployment rates were not associated with suicide rates.

Female labor force participation has been hypothesized to be associated with suicide rates because it might lead to role conflict and stress, both for men and for women (Stack, 1978). In the present study, the association was positive as predicted. However, suicide rates were also positively associated with male participation in the labor force and the overall participation in the labor force (the employment ratio), suggesting that the explanation for the association may be related employment *per se* rather than *female* employment and role conflict. Lester (1990a) found a similar pattern of associations over the states of America.

Muslim nations have some of the lowest reported suicide rates in the world (Conklin and Simpson, 1987), and the present study supported this association. Interestingly, Christianity (and in particular Roman Catholicism) was not associated with suicide rates.

There is a great deal of research linking alcohol use and abuse to suicidal behavior (Lester, 1992a). In the present analysis, nations with a higher per capita consumption of alcohol did have higher suicide rates as predicted.

It has recently been suggested that better medical resources may be associated with lower suicide rates because potential completed suicides are saved, thereby becoming attempted suicides (Lester, 1990b). In the present study, suicide rates were negatively associated with the numbers of hospital beds, nurses and physicians per capita (though only the two correlations were statistically significant), all in the direction predicted.

Wars appear to lower the suicide rate, and the military participation rate (the strength of the armed forces relative to the total population) has been found to be associated with the suicide rate (Lester, 1992b). In the present study, however, suicide rates were not associated with defense expenditures or the military participation rate.

Mawson and Jacobs (1978) noted that the synthesis of the neurotransmitter serotonin in the brain, the neurotransmitter thought to be responsible for depression, required the precursor amino acid L-tryptophan. Corn has less L-tryptophan than other cereals, and so people in nations with a higher corn consumption should have lower levels of serotonin and higher suicide rates. The present study found no support for such an association.

Lester (1981) speculated that ectomoprhy ratios of the residents of nations (that is, the height divided by the cube root of the weight) might be associated with suicide rates, since some research has found that the ectomorphy scores of individuals are associated with psychological disturbance. The present study found no support for this speculation.

The remaining associations found to be statistically significant in the present study were not expected and so explanations are not readily forthcoming: the rate of urban growth, illegitimate births, pharmacists per capita, the percentage of men in the population, and population growth rates.

SUICIDE AND HOMICIDE

The main theory linking suicide and homicide rates is that of Henry and Short (1954) which predicts that the social characteristics which increase the rate of one of these behaviors should decrease the rate of the other. Henry and Short saw suicide and homicide as reactions to frustration caused by there being, respectively, either few external causes to blame for one's misery or many external causes to blame for one's misery. Therefore, social conditions which lower one rate should increase the other rate (Lester, 1987).

In the present study, there were twenty social variables which were significantly associated with both suicide and homicide rates. All of these had one sign for suicide rates and the opposite sign for homicide rates! The variables were: gross domestic product per capita, quality of life (two measures), birth rates (three measures), infant mortality, life expectancy (two measures), marriage rates, the percentage of both the elderly and the young, the dependency ratio, illegitimate births, unionization, hospital beds per capita, caloric intake, male participation in the labor force, population growth rate, and alcohol consumption.

This remarkable result must be qualified by the fact that the suicide rate was significantly associated with fifteen other social variables which were not significantly associated with homicide rates (though thirteen of these fifteen were composed of pairs of associations with opposite signs), and the homicide rate was significantly associated with four variables which were not significantly associated with the suicide rate (though all four of these were composed of pairs of associations with opposite signs).

These results, therefore, provide strong support for Henry and Short's theory of the relationship between suicide and homicide rates and social variables.

OTHER THEORIES

In a recent ecological study of homicide rates over the states of America, Lester (1994) found that homicide rates were strongly associated with a measure of southern subculture, and less strongly with measures of social disintegration and labor force participation. In the present international study, of course, the notion of a southern subculture is inapplicable. However, homicide rates were negatively associated over nations with divorce rates (though not significantly) and alcohol consumption, a direction opposite to that found by Lester for the states of America. Homicide rates were negatively associated over nations with measures of labor force participation, a direction similar to that found by Lester for the states of America, but the associations failed to consistently reach statistical significance in the present study. Thus, the results found for the study of American states did not generalize to this international study.

A FACTOR ANALYSIS

In order to examine the associations further, the data set was subjected to a factor analysis using SPSS^X, with a principal components extraction and a varimax rotation, with pairwise deletion for missing values. Duplicate variables were eliminated from this analysis. Thirteen orthogonal factors were identified. Suicide had a high loading only on Factor 1, while homicide had a high loading only on Factor 12. These two factors are shown in Table 5.2.

Table 5.2 Factor Analysis Of The Data Set
(decimal points omitted, and only Factors 1 and 12 are shown)

	Factor	
	1	12
suicide	70*	09
quality of life	75*	-12
birth	-89*	27
% elderly	86*	-15
illegitimacy	-74*	40*
employment ratio	83*	16
female labor force	82*	17
dependence ratio	-86*	07
union strength	56*	05
hospital beds	-61*	02
% males	-70*	-22
population growth	-90*	03
male labor force	85*	-02
% under 15 years	-93*	09
height	45*	-05
alcohol consumption	74*	-14
caloric intake	80*	-15
% Muslim	-46*	-39
pharmacists/capita	50*	-19
gdp/capita	76*	-08
infant mortality	-50*	-07
life expectancy	64*	-15
urban growth	-76*	-11
literacy	75*	08
marriage	24	-10
% urban	31	-11
death rate	-12	-33
child labor	-32	19
doctors/capita	-28	25
nurses/capita	-38	-04
military participation rate	12	06
defense expenditures	-22	-08
defense expenditures/cap	05	-17

Table 5.2 (Continued)

weight	38	07
population	05	-17
area	08	25
corn consumption	-04	06
population density	10	11
ectomorphy	-03	-22
% Christian	33	13
% Roman Catholic	-09	16
divorce	16	-11
gnp growth	08	-05
strike days/capita	22	01
strikes/capita	21	-02
unemployment	-06	-07
political freedom	-26	-12
homicide	-34	74*
inflation	-05	-06
% of variance	35.7%	2.2%

On Factor 12, only the illegitimacy rate also had a high loading. In contrast, Factor 1 had twenty-three other variables with high loadings! Thus, the variables in this data set seem much more relevant to suicide than to homicide.

The variables loaded on Factor 1 along with the suicide rate were a mixed group in terms of content, including quality of life (quality of life, life expectancy, caloric intake and literacy), employment (male, female and total participation in the labor force), and age structure (birth rate, and percentages of the elderly and children).

Discussion

This preliminary analysis of the data set for nations of the world found many simple correlations between both the suicide and homicide rates and the social characteristics of the nations. Suicide rates had more significant associations with the social characteristics than did homicide rates, and more of the associations for suicide conformed to theory and previous research than the associations for homicide. However, one striking result was that the associations found between the social characteristics and homicide rates were in most cases opposite in direction to those found for suicide rates. Social conditions which increase the rate of one of these causes of death tend to decrease the rate of the other.

REFERENCES

Adrian, M. International trends in alcohol production, trade and consumption, and their relationship to alcohol-related problems, 1970 to 1977. *Journal of Public Health Policy,* 1984, 5, 344-367.

Barrett, D. B. *World Christian encyclopedia.* Oxford, England: Oxford University Press, 1982.

Conklin, G. H., & Simpson, M. E. The family, socioeconomic development and suicide. *Journal of Comparative Family Studies,* 1987, 18, 99-111.

Durkheim, E. *Le suicide.* Paris: Felix Alcan, 1897.

Estes, R. J. *The social progress of nations.* New York: Praeger, 1984.

Eveleth, P. B., & Tanner, J. M. *Worldwide variation in human growth.* New York: Cambridge University Press, 1976.

Gastil, R. D. *Freedom in the world.* New York: Freedom House, 1980.

Haas, M. Toward the study of biopolitics. *Behavioral Science,* 1969, 14, 257-280.

Henry, A. F., & Short, J. F. *Suicide and homicide.* Glencoe, IL: Free Press, 1954.

Johnson, B. D. Durkheim's one cause of suicide. *American Sociological Review,* 1965, 30, 875-886.

Kurian, G. T. *The new book of world rankings.* New York: Facts on File, 1984.

Lester, D. Ectomorphy and suicide. *Journal of Social Psychology,* 1981, 113, 135-136.

Lester, D. The association between the quality of life and suicide and homicide rates. *Journal of Social Psychology,* 1984, 124, 247-248.

Lester, D. Murder and suicide. *Behavioral Sciences & the Law,* 1987, 5, 49-60.

Lester, D. Strikes, suicide and homicide. *International Journal of Contemporary Sociology,* 1988, 25(1/2), 9-14.

Lester, D. Women in the labor force and suicide. *Psychological Reports,* 1990a, 66, 194.

Lester, D. Medical resources and suicide prevention. *Psychological Reports,* 1990b, 67, 344.

Lester, D. Alcoholism and drug abuse. In R. W. Maris, A. L. Berman, J. T. Maltsberger & R. I. Yufit (Eds.) *Assessment and prediction of suicide.* New York: Guilford, 1992a, 321-336.

Lester, D. War and personal violence. In G. Ausenda (Ed.) *Effects of war on society.* San Marino: AIEP, 1992b, 211-222.

Lester, D. *Patterns of suicide and homicide in America.* Commack, NY: Nova Science, 1994.

Lindgren, G. Measuring violations of the integrity of the person. *PIOOM Newsletter,* 1990, 2(2), 18-20.

Mawson, A., & Jacobs, K. Corn consumption, tryptophan and cross-national homicide rates. *Journal of Orthomolecular Psychiatry,* 1978, 7, 227-230.

Platt, S. D. Unemployment and suicidal behavior. *Social Science & Medicine,* 1984, 19, 93-115.

Stack, S. Suicide. *Social Forces,* 1978, 57, 644-653.

Stack, S. Domestic integration and the rate of suicide. *Journal of Comparative Family Studies,* 1980, 11, 249-260.

Stack, S. Suicide and religion. *Sociological Focus,* 1981, 14, 207-220.

Taylor, C. L., & Hudson, M. C. *World handbook of political and social indicators.* New Haven: Yale University, 1972.

Taylor, C. L., & Jodice, D. A. *World handbook of political and social indicators.* New Haven: Yale University, 1983.

United Nations. *Demographic yearbook.* New York: United Nations, 1986, 1990.

US Department of Agriculture. Reference tables on wheat, corn and total coarse grains supply-distribution for individual countries. *Foreign Agricultural Circular,* 1983, November 8, FG-19-83.

World Bank. *World development report.* New York: Oxford University Press, 1983a.

World Bank. *World Bank atlas.* Washington, DC: World Bank, 1983b.

World Bank. *World tables.* Baltimore, MD: Johns Hopkins University Press, 1983c.

World Bank. *World tables 1991.* Washington, DC: World Bank, 1991.

CHAPTER 6

PREDICTING NATIONAL SUICIDE AND HOMICIDE RATES

In the previous chapter, the social variables associated with suicide and homicide rates were identified. In the present chapter, the focus is instead on predicting the national suicide and homicide rates using the social variables, and both factor-analysis and regression analysis will be applied to this task.

A FACTOR-ANALYTIC APPROACH

The first step in this analysis was to subject the set of social variables to a factor-analysis in order to identify the basic factors (clusters of related social variables or social dimensions). Unfortunately, the data set had many missing values for some of the social variables. Initially, therefore, the social variables with the fewest missing values were entered into the factor-analysis (two or fewer missing values for the 72 nations in the total data set), eliminating duplicate variables. The list of social variables used is shown in Table 6.1.

Complete data (after listwise deletion) were available for 61 nations. The 22 social variables were subjected to a principal components extraction and a varimax rotation, and six orthogonal (independent) factors were identified (see Table 6.1).

Table 6.1

Factor-Analysis Of 22 Social Variables And Correlations With Suicide And Homicide Rates
(decimal points omitted from the factor loadings)

	Factor I	II	III	IV	V	VI
urban pop growth	72*	-33	26	23	-21	-09
% elderly	-84*	33	-10	-04	-08	-18
employment ratio	-87*	-02	16	-13	01	08
female labor force	-86*	-23	15	-09	08	16
dependency ratio	83*	-35	02	02	-07	-09
ratio of men/women	72*	06	45	-13	-05	-11
population growth	91*	-15	17	01	-06	-03
literacy	-68*	31	-23	-42	34	-01
birth rate	85*	-39	05	22	-09	-02
quality of life	-62*	42	-18	-47	38	-05
life expectancy	-60*	50*	-05	-45	31	-11
hospital beds/cap	57*	-51*	13	19	26	19
urban population	-22	84*	-06	-20	13	05
milit part rate	-18	53*	37	36	33	-03
% Christians	-30	17	-83*	-10	-09	-16
% Roman Catholics	19	04	-91*	01	06	-07
% Mulslim	47	25	61*	17	16	-09
political freedom	17	-02	01	81*	14	05
death rate	04	-28	11	69*	-52*	-02
gdp growth	-12	08	10	01	90*	-01
population	-04	-21	13	03	04	82*
area	-10	20	-02	02	-05	85*
% variance	43%	11%	10%	7%	6%	5%
Pearson Correlations						
suicide (n = 52)	-0.69#	0.03	0.07	0.10	0.02	0.05
homicide (n = 50)	0.36#	-0.27	-0.27	-0.13	0.05	0.05

* high factor loading (> 50)
\# significant at the two-tailed .05 level or better

The first factor had the highest loadings from high total population growth and high urban population growth, low participation in the labor force, few elderly people, a high birth rate, a high dependency ratio, and a high proportion of males. This seems to measure developing nation status. The second factor had high loadings from the gross domestic product per capita and urbanization; the third factor had high loadings from religion (fewer Christians, especially Roman Catholics, and more Muslims); the fourth factor had high loadings from the death rate and a political freedom index; the fifth factor had a high loading from the growth in the gross domestic product per capita; and the sixth and final factor had high loadings from the country's area and the population.

Suicide rates were strongly associated with scores on Factor I, while homicide rates were associated with scores on Factor I and almost significantly with scores on Factors II and III.

In order to explore this further, eight more social variables were added which had three or four missing values, reducing the sample size for the factor-analysis (after listwise deletion) to 54 nations. Seven orthogonal factors were identified, and now only scores from Factor I were associated with suicide and homicide rates (r = 0.64 for suicide rates and -0.46 for homicide rates). The social variables loaded on this factor included, in order of magnitude: the percentage of elderly, caloric intake, the gross domestic product per capita and the employment ratio positively and the percentage of children, the birth rate, population growth and dependency ratio negatively. This new factor seems to combine Factors I and II from the first analysis.

Adding five more social variables with up to 12 missing values further reduced the data set to 38 nations (after listwise deletion), and resulted in nine factors. Again, only scores from Factor I were associated with suicide and homicide rates (r = 0.65 for suicide rates and -0.57 for homicide rates). The social variables with high factor loadings now included: percentage of elderly, male participation in the labor force, caloric intake, and alcohol consumption positively and percentage of children, birth rate, dependency ratio and population growth negatively.

The conclusion seems to be that there are probably about six to nine independent factors of social variables, only one of which consistently correlates with suicide and homicide rates. Suicide rates are higher and homicide rates are lower in the more urban, wealthier and developed nations. Interestingly, suicide and homicide correlate in opposite direction with this factor score.

REGRESSION ANALYSES

Three regression analyses were carried out, using the three data sets in the three factor-analyses reported above. First, data from the 22 social variables with the fewest missing values were entered into a forward multiple regression analysis. Two social variables contributed significantly to the prediction of the suicide rate: birth rate (beta = -0.43) and female labor force participation (beta = 0.33), giving a multiple R of 0.69.

In contrast, five social variables contributed significantly to the prediction of the homicide rate: the dependency ratio (beta = 0.64), the percentage of males (beta = -0.33), the death rate (beta = -1.03), life expectancy (beta = -1.29) and the percentage of elderly (beta = 1.06), giving a multiple R of 0.80. Thus, though homicide rates were less strongly associated with the factors identified in the factor-analyses reported above, more social variables were associated with homicide rates than with suicide rates in the regression analsyes, and the resulting multiple R was higher for homicide rates.

Adding the next eight social variables to the data set, reducing the number of nations with complete data, changed the results of the regression analyses. Now only one social variable contributed significantly to the prediction of suicide rates, population growth (beta = -0.66), giving a multiple R of 0.66, while five social variables contributed significantly to the prediction of the homicide rates: dependency ratio (beta = 0.64), death rate (beta = -0.99) life expectancy (beta = -1.29), percentage of elderly (beta = 0.99) and the proportion of men (beta = -0.28), giving a multiple R of 0.82.

After adding the remaining five additional social variables to the data set, thereby reducing the sample size of nations with complete data still further, two social variables contributed significantly to the prediction of suicide rates: urban population growth (beta = -0.47) and the employment ratio (beta = 0.38), giving a multiple R of 0.79. Two social variables also contributed significantly to the prediction of homicide rates: literacy (beta = -0.86) and political freedom (beta = -0.45), giving a multiple R of 0.77.

DISCUSSION

Several features stand out in these results. First, only a limited number of factors are associated with suicide and homicide rates, usually one and occasionally two, depending upon the social variables included in the analyses. Thus, most of the social correlates of suicide and homicide rates identified in Chapter 5 are not independent correlates. Rather, they are strongly associated among themselves.

Second, though the associations between the factors scores and homicide rates were weaker than the correlations for suicide rates, more social variables contributed to the prediction of homicide rates in the regression equations, giving a greater multiple R for homicide rates.

Third, in all three factor analyses, the factor score which correlated with both suicide and homicide rates did so in opposite directions, supporting the proposition discussed in earlier chapters that suicide and homicide are polar opposites. However, the same social variables appeared too rarely in both the regression equations for suicide rates and for homicide rates for this "polar" hypothesis to be examined there.

CHAPTER 7

NATIONAL DIFFERENCES IN LETHAL VIOLENCE

Whitt, et al. (1972) argued that it might be of interest to explore social correlates of the total lethal aggression rate (the suicide rate plus the homicide rate) and the direction of aggression (the suicide rate divided by the lethal aggression rate). To explore whether these two measures of lethal aggression have different correlates from suicide and homicide rates alone, the associations were explored for the present data set. Data on both homicide and suicide rates were available for 57 nations. The results are shown in Table 7.1.

It can be seen that the lethal aggression rate was strongly associated with the homicide rate, yet was associated with very few of the social variables. Correlates of the direction of aggression rate were very similar to those for the suicide rate, though a little stronger in some cases. Thus, it would appear that, on the whole, the measures of lethal aggression and the direction of aggression add very little of substance to our understanding of personal violence.

In addition, Whitt argued that industrialization might increase the rate of suicide by generating frustration if the prevailing religious philosophy does not favor industrialization. Protestantism is fully congruent with the values involved in industrialization, Roman Catholicism does not contradict it, while non-Christain values seem opposed to it, according to Whitt. Thus, industrialization and the lethal aggression rate should be negatively related in Protestant nations, unrelated in Catholic nations and positively

Table 7.1

Correlates Of Lethal Aggression#

	lethal aggression	direction	suicide	homicide
lethal agg		-21	43*	83*
direction			62*	-62*
suicide				-15
illegitmacy	36*	-75*	-42*	60*
gdp/capita	-03	67*	55*	-36*
quality of life	-01	66*	55*	-33*
infant mortality	04	-71*	-52*	35*
life expectancy	-13	69*	47*	-42*
birth rate	16	-85*	-55*	50*
% elderly	02	77*	61*	-35*
% under 15	-04	-82*	-69*	38*
unionization	-07	50*	50*	-32*
hospitals	-03	-56*	-48*	27*
caloric intake	-12	71*	51*	-44*
alcohol consumpt	-01	60*	51*	-31*
employment ratio	14	63*	64*	-24
female labor force	20	57*	66*	-17
male labor force	06	68*	53*	-26
urban growth	-16	-57*	-56*	17
divorce	01	30*	35*	-21
child labor	04	-41*	-40*	27
nurses	03	-43*	-34*	24
pharmacists	03	46*	37*	-21
height	11	49*	41*	-21
literacy	19	52*	56*	-17
men/women	-26	-31*	-48*	01
% urban	-18	39*	17	-29*
doctors	09	-33*	-26	26*
% Roman Catholics	15	-30*	-17	27*
milit part ratio	-20	28*	02	-24
political rights	-02	-35*	-19	09
civil rights	04	-36*	-20	17
corn consumpt	05	-25	-07	10
gdp growth	-10	04	01	-12
population	-01	01	04	-03
marriage	-15	21	13	-24
population density	-03	18	05	-07
area	09	-04	14	01
inflation	-13	-03	-17	-06
unemployment	-03	02	03	-06
death rate	-16	-03	-04	-15
strike days	-08	25	06	-11
strikes	04	23	30	-10
weight	19	29	32	-05
ectomorphy	-17	18	05	-21
% Christians	18	01	12	13
% Muslims	-26	-09	-26	-12
defense expend	-23	-01	-19	-14

decimal points omitted
* significant at the 5% level or better

related in non-Christian nations. Whitt used the percentage of economically active males not engaged in agriculture as a measure of industrialization, and the present analyses used a similar measure obtained from the World Bank (1991). The present study defined a Roman Catholic nations as one where more than 80 percent of the members were Catholic, a Protestant nation as one where more than 80 percent of the members were Protestant (a stricter criterion than that used by Whitt), and a non-Christian nation as one where less than 20% of the residents were Christian.

The results of the analysis (see Table 7.2) did not support Whitt's predictions since all of the correlations between the lethal aggression rate and the percentage engaged in agriculture were not significantly different from zero.

Table 7.2 Correlations Between Aggression Rates And The Percentage Engaged In Agriculture

	suicide	homicide	lethal aggress	direction of aggress	n
Roman Catholic nations	-0.64**	0.58**	0.38	-0.78***	20
Protestant nations	0.15	0.74	0.23	-0.47	7
non-Christian nations	0.09	0.54	0.43	-0.37	11
all nations	-0.34*	0.40**	0.18	-0.62***	54

* two-tailed p < .05
** two-tailed p < .01
*** two-tailed p < .001

Whitt felt that Protestantism stressed individual initiative and psychological punishment, leading to a higher suicide rate/lethal aggression rate ratio than Catholic and non-Christian nations. In fact, the lethal aggression rate for the seven Protestant nations was 17.70 (sd = 9.22), for the twenty-one Catholic nations 20.81 (sd = 23.28) and for the eleven other nations 12.15 (sd = 11.09). Thus, Whitt's hypothesis was not supported.

Finally, Whitt felt that industrialization weakens external restraints on behavior, and so the direction of aggression measure should be positively related to industrialization. The results are shown in Table 7.2 where the correlations between the percentage of people engaged in agriculture and the direction of aggression measure can be seen to be negative for all groups of nations, as predicted. In particular, homicide rates seem to be higher in general and the suicide rates somewhat lower in the more agricultural nations.

Thus, only one of Whitt three hypotheses was supported in the present replication.

Pockets of Violence

Lester (1985) approached the regional study of suicide and homicide by classifying cities as high/low in suicide and high/low in homicide, giving four types of cities -- violent, nonviolent, inwardly-violent and outwardly-violent. For the present analysis, nations were classified into these four types, and the social charatceristics of the four types of nations were explored. Data on both homicide and suicide rates were available for 57 nations.

The nations were divided as high/low in suicide and homicide by means of median splits. The nations are shown in Table 7.3, together with the significant differences in social characteristics.[6]

The nations low in both kinds of violence were Muslim, with a large military, high total population growth and urban population growth and a relatively high birth rate. Nations high in both kinds of violence had high marriage and divorce rates, high female labor force participation, a large area, and weak political and civil rights.

Nations with high suicide and low homicide rates were economically strong, with a high quality of life, caloric intake, life expectancy, literacy and political freedom, very urban, unionized and with a large elderly population. Nations with high homicide and low suicide rates had high birth rates, infant mortality rates, illegitimacy rates, men/women ratios, and nurses per capita and little political and civil freedoms.

6 The four groups of nations did not differ significantly in population, population density, death rates, the percentage of Christians or Roman Catholics, inflation, unemployment, corn consumption, doctors per capita, ectomorphy ratios, growth in the gnp, child labor or political freedom.

Table 7.3

Nations High And Low In Suicide And Homicide#

Type A	Type B	Type C	Type D
Egypt	Brazil	Austria	Bulgaria
Greece	Chile	Belgium	Canada
Ireland	Costa Rica	Czech	El Salvador
Israel	Colombia	Denmark	Finland
Italy	Ecuador	France	Hungary
Kuwait	Guatemala	Hong Kong	Puerto Rico
Papua	Honduras	Japan	Sri Lanka
Peru	India	Netherlands	USA
Saudi Arabia	Jordan	N Zealand	USSR
Spain	Mexico	Norway	Yugoslavia
Syria	Panama	Poland	
	Paraguay	Portugal	
	S Africa	Sweden	
	Thailand	Switzerland	
	Trinidad	UK	
	Venezuela	W Germany	
	Zimbabwe		

	A	B	C	D	ANOVA F	p<
Muslim	27*	6	0	4	3.67	.02
defense exp	93*	33	29	34	3.76	.02
milit part	129*	48	74	94	2.93	.05
urban growth	43*	38	14	25	12.14	.0001
pop growth	26*	27*	8	12	13.80	.001
men/women	508*	504*	490	491	5.13	.004
fertility	44*	47*	18	25	16.48	.001
infant mort	488	584*	119	268	9.88	.0001
birth rate	253	309*	138	197	11.09	.0001
illeg births	92	407*	90	180	9.20	.0001
hospitals	347	562	110	200	9.90	.0001
nurses	675	1285*	226	376	5.51	.003
% under 15	364	415*	228	269	28.21	.0001
polit rights	3.6	4.0*	1.9	4.0*	3.66	.02
civil rights	3.4	3.8*	1.8	3.8*	4.38	.009
gdp/capita	2933	1904	5637*	4124	17.59	.001
qual of life	122	102	174*	140	16.62	.0001
life expect	661	637	740*	695	9.41	.0001
% urban	607	500	747*	538	4.66	.007
% elderly	72	36	127*	85	24.99	.0001
employ ratio	331	326	465*	435	16.57	.0001
unionization	33	18	44*	32	4.01	.02
calories	3008	2409	3383*	3187	17.87	.0001
alc consumpt	484	290	905*	676	7.48	.0004
literacy	62	77	97*	91	10.14	.0001
fem lab force	221	252	388*	385*	13.35	.0001
marriage	67	61	67	81*	3.00	.05
divorce	95	47	184	236*	7.65	.0005
area	575	1155	201	4721	3.83	.02
height	1437	1394	1471	1489*	11.86	.0001
weight	364	323	378	398*	6.23	.003

decimal points omitted from variable scores
* group with highest score on the variable

As Lester (1985) pointed out, this type of analysis eliminates the danger of oversimplification that can result from simple correlational analyses and suggests that a typology based on the total amount and direction of personal violence in a culture may be useful.

DISCUSSION

Although Whitt's suggestion of studying the lethal violence rate of regions and the direction in which this lethal violence is directed proved to be of little use in furthering our understanding of the regional variation in suicide and homicide rates, Lester's suggestion of classifying regions by the direction and type of aggression (that is, classifying nations into violent, nonviolent, outwardly violent and inwardly violent nations) produced interesting results which merit further study.

REFERENCES

Lester, D. Regional variation in suicide and homicide. *Suicide & Life-Threatening Behavior*, 1985, 15, 110-116.

Whitt, H. P., Gordon, C. C., & Hofley, J. R. Religion, economic development and lethal aggression. *American Sociological Review*, 1972, 37, 193-201.

World Bank. *World Tables, 1991*. Washington, DC: World Bank, 1991.

CHAPTER 8

CHANGES IN SUICIDE AND HOMICIDE RATES

So far in this volume, we have explored how well social indicators in 1980 predict suicide and homicide rates also in 1980. Sainsbury, et al. (1980) explored how well social indicators in one year and changes in these social indicators over the following decade predicted changes in suicide rates over the following decade for eighteen European nations.

The present study was designed to explore these issues for the total sample of nations examined in this volume. Data were obtained for 1970 for the following variables (from the same sources used for the 1980 values): the real gross domestic product per capita, the quality of life, the population, female labor force participation, the percentage of the urban population, the percentage of the population under 15 years of age, the divorce rate, the birth rate and the marriage rate. Since the suicide rate of two nations in 1970 was zero (Egypt and Iraq), only absolute changes in the suicide rate could be explored. However, in addition to Pearson correlation coefficients, partial correlation coefficients controlling for the suicide rate in 1970 were also calculated, and a similar analysis conducted for homicide rates even though no nation had a zero homicide rate in 1970.

The results are shown in Table 8.1, where it can be seen that the social indicators were quite unsuccessful in predicting changes in suicide rates from 1970 to 1980. The 1970 quality of life was positively associated with

Table 8.1

Predicting Changes In Suicide And Homicide Rates From 1970 To 1980

1970 measure and changes from 1970 to 1980	changes in suicide rates Pearson r	Partial r	homicide rate Pearson r	Partial r
gdp/capita	0.18	-0.12	-0.33*	0.04
absolute change	0.18	-0.02	-0.31*	0.09
percentage change	-0.08	-0.09	-0.19	-0.14
quality of life	0.37*	0.16	-0.29	0.28
absolute change	-0.07	-0.05	0.01	-0.06
percentage change	-0.09	-0.06	0.02	-0.06
population	-0.11	-0.17	-0.06	-0.09
absolute change	-0.06	-0.08	-0.04	-0.08
percentage change	0.22	0.22	-0.01	0.04
female labor force	0.27	-0.07	-0.28	-0.10
absolute change	-0.01	0.08	0.05	0.06
percentage change	-0.19	0.06	0.29	0.09
urban population	-0.10	-0.27	-0.25	0.03
absolute change	0.04	0.09	-0.19	-0.10
percentage change	-0.08	0.01	-0.12	-0.13
% children	-0.29	0.06	0.39*	-0.18
absolute change	-0.02	0.03	0.02	0.05
percentage change	-0.11	0.02	0.11	-0.01
divorce rate	0.12	-0.13	-0.19	-0.30
absolute change	-0.07	-0.13	-0.22	-0.06
percentage change#	-0.07	-0.02	-0.11	0.09
birth rate	-0.26	-0.02	0.47*	-0.10
absolute change	-0.01	-0.11	0.16	0.03
percentage change	-0.12	-0.17	0.20	-0.05
marriage rate	0.11	-0.09	-0.52*	-0.34*
absolute change	-0.11	0.01	0.34*	0.05
percentage change	-0.06	0.06	0.47*	0.14

* two-tailed p < .05 or better
# Three nations were excluded from this one analysis because they had zero divorce rates in 1970 (Ireland, Italy and Spain)

absolute changes in the suicide rate from 1970 to 1980, but not after the 1970 suicide rate was controlled for by means of partial correlation coefficients.

The social indicators were only a little more successful in predicting changes in the homicide rates. The gross domestic product per capita in 1970 and changes from 1970 to 1980 were associated with absolute changes in the homicide rate, as were the percentage of young people in 1970, the birth rate in 1970, and the marriage rate in 1970 (and absolute and percentage changes in the marriage rate). However, after controls for the 1970 homicide rate by means of partial correlation coefficients, only the correlation with the 1970 marriage rate remained statistically significant.

Thus, the present chapter indicates that the small set of social indicators examined here were only minimally associated with changes in the suicide and homicide rates from 1970 to 1980. Clearly, more effective predictors of such changes must be sought for in future research.

References

Sainsbury, P., Jenkins, J., & Levey, A. The social correlates of suicide in Europe. In R. Farmer & S. Hirsch (Eds.) *The suicide syndrome*. London: Croom Helm, 1980, 38-53.

CHAPTER 9

CHANGES IN THE METHODS USED FOR SUICIDE FROM 1960 TO 1980[7]

Occasional reports have appeared documenting changes in the use of methods for suicide in one country. For example, Boyd (1983) commented on the increasing use of firearms for suicide in the USA from 1953 to 1978.

Reports have appeared also on the effects of a change in the suicidal environment on the methods used for suicide. Clarke and Lester (1989) documented how the detoxification of domestic gas in England and Wales was accompanied by the virtual elimination of suicide by domestic gas and, incidentally, a lowering of the overall suicide rate.

Farmer and Rhode (1980) noted that the individuals committing suicide in different nations of the world choose different methods. They reported comparative data on the use of different methods for suicide in various nations of the world for one time period, but no study has yet appeared on how the use of methods for suicide has *changed* over time for a sample of nations of the world. The present analysis was designed to explore these changes.

The suicide rates by each method of suicide for 1960-1964 for 16 nations were obtained from a report of the World Health Organization (1973). Suicide rates by each method for nations of the world in 1980 were calculated by the present author from data provided by members of the International Association for Suicide Prevention and from colleagues in various nations

7 A version of this chapter appeared in Lester (1990b).

(Lester, 1990c). The total set of rates obtained by Lester is shown in Table 9.1 and the data examined for the present study in Table 9.2.

The changes in suicide rates by each method for suicide during the period under study are shown in Table 9.3. The overall suicide rate rose for this sample of 16 nations rose from a mean of 11.8 per 100,000 per year in 1960-1964 to a mean of 14.8 in 1980.

Looking at each method for suicide, it can be seen that the suicide rate by domestic gas has decreased and, in fact, has been virtually eliminated. During the 1960s and 1970s, most countries in the present sample which had been using coal gas, which is toxic because of the carbon monoxide in it, have switched to natural gas which is far less toxic.

During the period, there were significant increases in suicide by "other gas" (which is mainly motor vehicle exhaust), hanging, firearms, jumping and "other methods". Interestingly, suicide by poisons (solids and liquids), drowning and by cutting/piercing did not increase significantly during the period.

Some of the changes for individual countries are readily explained. Restrictions of lethal medications in Australia and Japan during this period have been documented (Lester and Abe, 1989; Oliver and Hetzel, 1972), but such analyses have not appeared for all of the nations experiencing changes in the suicide rate by solid and liquid substances. Similarly, Clarke and Lester (1989) have documented changes in the suicide rate by motor vehicle exhaust, but only for the USA and for England and Wales.

The present data indicate that although the suicide rates of nations are quite stable, with the relative rankings of nations remaining much the same over time, changes within nations in the methods used for suicide are quite extensive. People in nations clearly switch methods for suicide, perhaps in response to the changing availability of these methods in their environment as suggested by Clarke and Lester (1989). Studying just one method for suicide, Lester (1990a) has shown that the availability of guns in nations seems to be related to their use for suicide. Studies on the availability of other methods for suicide in a sample of nations of the world would be most useful in explaining the varying use of different methods for suicide both between nations and over time.

Table 9.1

List Of Suicide Rates By Method In 1980

	total	E950	E951	E952	E953	E954	E955	E956	E957	E958	E959
Australia	10.94	2.79	0.19	1.39	1.46	0.37	3.52	0.18	0.42	0.61	0.01
Austria	25.59	3.91	0.01	1.30	12.64	1.13	3.13	0.41	1.88	1.19	0.00
Belgium	22.04	4.49	0.08	0.23	9.00	3.27	2.62	0.24	1.32	0.77	0.01
Brazil	3.21	0.66	0.00	0.01	1.07	0.08	0.54	0.07	0.06	0.71	0.00
Canada	13.97	2.63	0.01	1.49	3.11	0.76	4.66	0.22	0.60	0.47	0.01
Costa Rica	4.27	------	1.07	------	1.11	0.00	1.64	0.13	0.31	0.00	0.00
Denmark	31.57	9.86	0.90	3.03	9.57	2.77	2.50	0.51	1.29	1.15	0.00
England	8.71	3.17	0.02	0.95	2.14	0.70	0.44	0.21	0.39	0.67	0.00
Finland	25.65	4.02	0.08	1.09	9.21	1.72	6.74	0.40	1.09	1.28	0.04
France	19.37	2.44	0.05	0.26	7.27	2.19	4.16	0.14	1.03	1.83	0.00
Germany W	20.90	5.09	0.04	1.18	8.94	1.07	1.30	0.32	1.35	1.61	0.00
Hungary	44.90	12.74	0.97	0.00	24.53	1.91	0.63	0.67	1.92	1.52	0.00
Iceland	10.52	1.75	0.00	2.19	1.32	2.63	1.32	0.00	0.88	0.00	0.44
Ireland	6.35	1.56	0.32	0.21	1.59	1.76	0.56	0.18	0.12	0.06	0.00
Israel	5.96	0.90	0.00	0.00	1.55	0.15	1.68	0.15	1.08	0.44	0.00
Italy	7.36	0.68	0.12	0.12	2.63	0.78	0.96	0.11	1.63	0.35	0.00
Japan	17.55	1.14	0.91	1.09	9.37	1.32	0.08	0.44	1.17	2.03	0.00
Nether.	11.01	2.30	0.04	0.17	3.92	1.87	0.22	0.16	0.92	1.42	0.00
N Zealand	10.83	1.70	0.10	1.93	2.63	0.87	2.12	0.29	0.93	0.26	0.00
Norway	12.39	2.96	0.00	0.61	3.28	1.20	3.06	0.34	0.46	0.46	0.02
Poland*	13.19	0.60	0.87	0.00	9.48	0.48	0.08	0.22	0.75	0.37	0.00
Scotland	9.99	3.57	0.02	0.97	2.29	1.34	0.52	0.19	0.72	0.37	0.00
Singapore	16.30	------	1.87	------	3.80	0.16	0.16	0.11	9.99	0.16	0.00
S Africa	4.30	0.38	---0.46	---	1.80	0.02	1.44	0.01	0.05	0.14	0.00
Spain	4.41	0.28	0.01	0.03	2.11	0.36	0.33	0.05	0.52	0.73	0.00
Sweden	19.37	4.06	0.29	1.84	6.96	1.64	2.29	0.37	1.10	0.82	0.02
Switz.	25.39	3.56	0.06	2.22	6.84	2.55	5.04	0.49	2.46	2.10	0.00
Turkey	1.67	0.27	---0.01	---	0.85	0.27	0.01	0.01	0.13	0.11	0.00
USA	11.80	1.33	0.02	1.05	1.62	0.24	6.76	0.17	0.38	0.22	0.01
Venezuela	4.80	0.89	0.00	0.00	2.20	0.02	1.04	0.15	0.39	0.11	0.01
Yugoslav	14.70	------	1.23	------	9.28	1.14	0.93	0.39	0.50	1.23	0.00

* The individual rates do not add up to the total rate

E950 solids/liquids
E951 domestic gas
E952 other gases (mainly motor vehicle exhaust)
E953 hanging, strangulation, suffocation
E954 submersion (drowning)
E955 firearms, explosives
E956 cutting, piercing
E957 jumping
E958 other and unspecified
E959 late effects of self-inflicted injury

Table 9.2

Rates Of Suicide By Each Method For Nations Of The World: 1960-1964 (first row) And 1980 (second row)

	total	E950	E951	E952	E953	E954	E955	E956	E957	E958
Australia	13.4	4.8	1.6	0.9	1.6	0.6	3.0	0.3	0.2	0.3
	10.9	2.8	0.2	1.4	1.5	0.4	3.5	0.2	0.4	0.6
Belgium	14.2	0.9	1.6	0.1	7.6	2.3	0.6	0.2	0.3	0.6
	22.0	4.5	0.1	0.2	9.0	3.3	2.6	0.2	1.3	0.8
Canada	7.6	1.2	0.0	0.7	1.7	0.6	2.9	0.2	0.2	0.2
	14.0	2.6	0.0	1.5	3.1	0.8	4.7	0.2	0.6	0.5
Denmark	19.2	5.6	3.9	0.4	5.9	1.4	1.2	0.2	0.5	0.3
	31.6	9.9	0.9	3.0	9.6	2.8	2.5	0.5	1.3	1.2
England & Wales	11.7	3.1	5.1	0.3	1.2	0.8	0.4	0.2	0.2	0.4
	8.7	3.2	0.0	0.9	2.1	0.7	0.4	0.2	0.4	0.7
France	15.5	0.9	0.9	0.1	8.0	2.2	1.7	0.2	0.3	1.2
	19.4	2.4	0.1	0.3	7.3	2.2	4.2	0.1	1.0	1.8
Germany (West)	19.1	2.3	2.1	2.0	8.2	1.4	0.8	0.3	0.9	1.1
	20.9	5.1	0.0	1.2	8.9	1.1	1.3	0.3	1.4	1.6
Italy	5.5	0.6	0.4	0.0	1.8	0.7	0.7	0.1	0.8	0.3
	7.4	0.7	0.1	0.1	2.6	0.8	1.0	0.1	1.6	0.4
Japan	18.0	6.2	0.8	0.0	6.6	1.9	0.1	0.3	0.3	1.7
	17.6	1.1	0.9	1.1	9.4	1.3	0.1	0.4	1.2	2.0
Netherlands	6.5	0.8	1.4	0.0	2.3	1.3	0.1	0.1	0.2	0.3
	11.0	2.3	0.0	0.2	3.9	1.9	0.2	0.2	0.9	1.4
New Zealand	8.8	2.2	1.0	0.8	1.2	0.9	1.9	0.4	0.3	0.2
	10.8	1.7	0.1	1.9	2.6	0.9	2.1	0.3	0.9	0.3
Norway	7.3	1.2	0.1	0.1	2.7	1.0	1.6	0.2	0.3	0.1
	12.4	3.0	0.0	0.6	3.3	1.2	3.1	0.3	0.5	0.5
Scotland	8.3	2.2	3.4	0.1	0.8	0.8	0.3	0.2	0.2	0.3
	10.0	3.6	0.0	1.0	2.3	1.3	0.5	0.2	0.7	0.4
Switzerland	18.0	1.9	2.0	0.5	5.3	2.1	3.8	0.3	1.1	1.1
	25.4	3.6	0.1	2.2	6.8	2.6	5.0	0.5	2.5	2.1
USA	10.7	1.5	0.1	1.1	1.7	0.3	5.1	0.2	0.4	0.3
	11.8	1.3	0.0	1.1	1.6	0.2	6.8	0.2	0.4	0.2
Venezuela	5.6	1.6	0.0	0.0	2.0	0.0	1.3	0.1	0.4	0.2
	4.8	0.9	0.0	0.0	2.2	0.0	1.0	0.2	0.4	0.1

Table 9.3

Changes In The Suicide Rates From 1960-1964 To 1980

	1960-1964		1980		
	mean	(SD)	mean	(SD)	t (df=15)
overall	11.84	(4.99)	14.92	(7.25)	3.01*
solids/liquids	2.31	(1.75)	3.04	(2.22)	1.30
domestic gas	1.53	(1.50)	0.16	(0.30)	-3.73*
other gas	0.44	(0.55)	1.04	(0.83)	3.04*
hanging etc	3.66	(2.74)	4.76	(3.12)	4.02*
submersion	1.14	(0.69)	1.34	(0.96)	1.59
firearms etc	1.59	(1.44)	2.44	(1.99)	3.92*
cutting etc	0.22	(0.08)	0.26	(0.12)	1.38
jumping	0.41	(0.28)	0.97	(0.57)	5.78*
other methods	0.54	(0.47)	0.91	(0.67)	4.12*

* significant at the 1% level (two-tailed) or better.

References

Boyd, J. The increasing rate of suicide by firearms. *New England Journal of Medicine*, 1983, 308, 872-874.

Clarke, R. V., & Lester, D. *Suicide: closing the exits*. New York: Springer-Verlag, 1989.

Farmer, R., & Rhode, J. R. Effect of availability and acceptability of lethal instruments on suicide mortality. *Acta Psychiatrica Scandinavica*, 1980, 62, 436-446.

Lester, D. The availability of firearms and the use of firearms for suicide. *Acta Psychiatrica Scandinavica*, 1990a, 81, 146-147.

Lester, D. Changes in the methods used for suicide in 16 countries from 1960 to 1980. *Acta Psychiatrica Scandinavica*, 1990b, 81, 260-261.

Lester, D. Suicide rates arond the world. *Crisis*, 1990c, 11, 82-84.

Lester, D, & Abe, K. The effects of controls on sedatives and hypnotics and their use for suicide. *Clinical Toxicology*, 1989, 27, 299-303.

Oliver, R. G., & Hetzel, B. S. Rise and fall of suicide rates in Australia. *Medical Journal of Australia*, 1972, 2, 919-923.

World Health Organization. Suicide. *World Health Statistical Reports*, 1973, 26(3), 114-281.

CHAPTER 10

GENDER DIFFERENCES IN SUICIDE AND HOMICIDE RATES

There have been many differences by gender observed in national suicide and homicide rates, and in this chapter we will examine some of these differences.

Verkko's Hypothesis

Verkko (1951) argued that, in nations where homicide was more common, this was due to the greater involvement of male victims. In addition, in nations where the homicide rate was changing, this was due mainly to changes in the participation of males. Lester (1973) confirmed the first hypothesis in a study of thirty-three nations.

The present analysis used data from 1980 to check upon the validity of the first part of Verkko's hypothesis. The data are shown in Table 10.1. The Pearson correlation between the total homicide rate and the ratio of the male/female homicide rates was 0.68 (two-tailed $p < .001$). Thus, in nations where the homicide rate was higher, the male homicide rate was relatively higher than the female homicide rate, confirming Verkko's hypothesis.

No one has yet investigated Verkko's hypothesis to see whether it applies also to suicide. Analysis of the data set in Table 10.1 indicated that

Table 10.1

Suicide Rates By Sex In Nations Of The World In 1979-1981

	Suicide				Homicide			
	total	male	female	m/f ratio	total	male	female	m/f ratio
Argentina	7.2	9.7	4.3	2.26	3.7	5.3	1.9	2.79
Australia	11.3	16.6	5.9	2.81	1.9	2.4	1.3	1.85
Austria	26.0	38.3	14.9	2.57	1.3	1.3	1.2	1.08
Belgium	21.5	28.2	15.0	1.88	1.6	1.8	1.4	1.29
Brazil	3.4	4.7	2.1	2.24	11.5	20.8	2.3	9.04
Bulgaria	13.9	19.4	8.3	2.34	2.7	4.2	1.3	3.23
Canada	14.1	21.3	6.9	3.09	2.3	3.0	1.6	1.87
Chile	5.5	9.3	1.8	5.17	2.7	4.5	0.9	5.00
Costa Rica	4.4	7.0	1.7	4.12	4.7	7.6	1.9	4.00
Czechoslovak	19.8	30.3	9.9	3.06	1.1	1.2	1.0	1.20
Denmark	29.1	37.3	21.1	1.77	1.2	1.2	1.3	0.92
Ecuador	2.8	3.5	2.1	1.67	6.0	10.5	1.4	7.50
Egypt	0.1	0.1	0.05	2.00	0.8	1.3	0.3	4.30
El Salvador	9.7	14.7	4.6	3.20	37.6	67.6	7.4	9.14
Finland	24.7	40.4	10.0	4.04	2.9	4.3	1.5	2.87
France	19.2	27.9	10.9	2.56	1.0	1.3	0.8	1.62
Germany, West	21.4	29.0	14.4	2.01	1.2	1.3	1.0	1.30
Greece	3.2	4.4	2.0	2.20	0.7	1.1	0.4	2.75
Guatemala	1.0	1.8	0.2	9.00	64.4	118.8	10.9	10.90
Honduras	1.2	2.1	0.4	5.25	9.5	17.2	1.7	10.12
Hong Kong	12.4	13.5	11.1	1.22	1.5	2.2	0.8	2.75
Hungary	45.0	63.9	27.3	2.34	2.5	3.0	1.9	1.58
Ireland	6.2	8.7	3.7	2.35	1.2	1.6	0.8	2.00
Israel	6.0	7.8	4.1	1.90	1.8	2.5	1.1	2.27
Italy	7.1	9.9	4.3	2.30	1.8	3.0	0.7	4.29
Japan	17.5	22.2	13.0	1.71	1.0	1.1	0.8	1.37
Kuwait	0.7	0.9	0.5	1.80	0.9	1.0	0.7	1.43
Mexico	1.7	2.6	0.7	3.71	17.5	31.9	3.0	10.63
Netherlands	10.2	12.3	8.1	1.52	0.8	1.1	0.5	2.20
New Zealand	10.2	14.5	5.9	2.46	1.4	1.6	1.1	1.45
Norway	12.4	18.2	6.7	2.72	1.1	1.5	0.8	1.87
Panama	2.0	3.3	0.6	5.50	2.3	3.8	0.7	5.43
Papua-New Guin	0.2	0.1	0.2	0.50	0.1	0.2	0.1	2.00
Paraguay	2.7	3.0	2.4	1.25	9.5	17.2	1.9	9.05
Poland	12.7	21.8	4.0	5.45	1.0	1.3	0.7	1.86
Portugal	8.3	12.5	4.5	2.78	1.4	2.1	0.6	3.50
Puerto Rico	8.5	14.6	2.7	5.41	14.6	26.9	2.8	9.61
Singapore	9.8	10.8	8.9	1.21	1.9	2.7	1.1	2.45
South Africa	5.3	8.4	2.2	3.82	22.5	38.1	6.3	6.05
Spain	4.4	6.6	2.2	3.00	1.0	1.6	0.4	4.00
Sri Lanka	29.0	37.7	19.7	1.91	2.3	3.9	0.6	6.50
Sweden	19.1	26.8	11.6	2.31	1.3	1.6	1.0	1.60
Switzerland	24.7	34.9	15.0	2.33	1.0	0.9	1.1	0.82
Thailand	7.1	7.4	6.9	1.07	25.8	45.8	5.4	8.48
Trinidad & T	4.8	7.0	2.6	2.69	3.3	4.3	2.4	1.79
United Kingdom	8.7	11.0	6.5	1.69	1.0	1.1	0.7	1.57
USA	12.0	18.6	5.7	3.26	10.2	16.4	4.4	3.73
Venezuela	4.7	7.6	1.9	4.00	11.2	20.6	1.7	12.12
Yugoslavia	14.8	21.0	8.8	2.39	2.1	2.9	1.2	2.42
Zimbabwe	6.1	9.9	2.6	3.81	16.7	29.2	5.4	5.41

Table 10.2

Percentage Changes In The Suicide And Homicide Rates From 1969-1971 to 1979-1981

	suicide				homicide			
	total	male	female	test*	total	male	female	test*
Argentina	-28%	-37%	-10%	YES	-49%	-56%	-21%	YES
Australia	-11%	-3%	-28%	NO	+27%	+26%	+8%	YES
Austria	+13%	+17%	+3%	YES	0%	-19%	+9%	-
Belgium	+37%	+31%	+49%	NO	+60%	+80%	+56%	YES
Bulgaria	+18%	+20%	+9%	YES	+4%	+8%	0%	YES
Canada	+24%	+31%	+10%	YES	+15%	+15%	+14%	YES
Chile	-11%	-7%	-28%	NO	-31%	-37%	0%	YES
Costa Rica	+57%	+37%	+183%	NO	+21%	+25%	+19%	YES
Czechoslov	-18%	-16%	-24%	NO	-21%	-29%	-9%	YES
Denmark	+30%	+31%	+29%	YES	+50%	+50%	+86%	NO
Ecuador	+22%	+6%	+62%	NO	-17%	-20%	0%	YES
El Salvador	+28%	+11%	+119%	NO	+93%	+22%	+90%	NO
Finland	+12%	+13%	+5%	YES	+21%	+19%	+7%	YES
France	+24%	+22%	+27%	NO	+25%	+30%	+33%	NO
Germany W	+2%	+4%	-3%	YES	-8%	-19%	0%	YES
Greece	-3%	-6%	0%	YES	+17%	+18%	0%	YES
Guatemala	-69%	-63%	-86%	NO	+219%	+224%	+203%	YES
Hong Kong	+17%	+15%	+18%	NO	0%	-4%	+33%	-
Hungary	+30%	+27%	+37%	NO	+19%	+11%	+27%	NO
Ireland	+195%	+172%	+270%	NO	+200%	+220%	+300%	NO
Israel	-9%	+4%	-27%	NO	-71%	-78%	+22%	YES
Italy	+25%	+24%	+23%	YES	+100%	+150%	+40%	YES
Japan	+16%	+30%	-1%	YES	-30%	-39%	-11%	YES
Mexico	+112%	+86%	+133%	NO	+24%	+23%	+30%	NO
Netherlands	+29%	+28%	+31%	NO	+60%	+57%	+25%	YES
New Zealand	+10%	+21%	-11%	YES	+27%	+23%	+22%	YES
Norway	+51%	+47%	+63%	NO	+83%	+67%	+100%	NO
Panama	-37%	-39%	-33%	YES	-34%	-28%	-59%	NO
Paraguay	+80%	+58%	+118%	NO	+44%	+43%	+36%	YES
Poland	+11%	+15%	-2%	YES	-9%	-7%	0%	YES
Portugal	+4%	-3%	+32%	NO	+56%	+75%	0%	YES
Puerto Rico	-12%	0%	-47%	NO	+18%	+27%	-32%	YES
Singapore	+1%	-4%	+11%	NO	+6%	-7%	+83%	NO
Spain	+2%	0%	+5%	NO	+233%	+220%	+100%	YES
Sri Lanka	+53%	+50%	+81%	NO	-	-	-	-
Sweden	-11%	-12%	-9%	YES	+44%	+45%	+43%	YES
Switzerland	+36%	+33%	+44%	NO	+67%	+29%	+83%	NO
Thailand	+82%	+68%	+109%	NO	+51%	+50%	+46%	YES
Trinidad & T	-8%	-16%	+30%	YES	-15%	-19%	0%	YES
United King	+7%	+13%	-2%	YES	+43%	+22%	0%	YES
USA	+5%	+13%	-12%	YES	+23%	+21%	+26%	NO
Venezuela	-31%	-20%	-54%	NO	+42%	+48%	0%	YES
Yugoslavia	+6%	+3%	+16%	NO	-38%	-45%	-25%	YES
Zimbabwe	+2%	+4%	+8%	NO	-	-	-	-

* fit with Verkko's hypothesis

the total suicide rate was not significantly associated with the male/female suicide rate ratio ($r = -0.20$, not significant). Thus, Verkko's hypothesis is not valid for suicide rates.

Interestingly, the mean male/female suicide rate ratio for the 50 nations (2.83) was significantly smaller than the mean male/female homicide rate ratio (4.06: $t_{49} = 3.06$, two-tailed $p < .01$). This means that the difference in the male and female suicide rates was less than the difference in the male and female homicide rates.

Incidentally, the suicide rates of the nations of the world were significantly higher than the homicide rates (11.10 versus 6.39, $t_{49} = 2.02$, $p = .05$). The female suicide rates were higher than the female homicide rates (6.62 versus 1.84, $t_{49} = 5.01$, $p < .001$) but the male rates did not differ significantly (15.67 versus 10.96, $t_{49} = 1.22$).

Changes in the Homicide and Suicide Rates

To investigate the second part of Verkko's hypothesis, the percentage changes in the homicide and suicide rates from 1969-1971 to 1979-1981 were calculated overall and for men and women separately. If Verkko's hypothesis is correct, the percentage change for the male homicide rate (in the same direction as the change in the overall homicide rate) should be greater than the percentage change for the female homicide rate. The data are shown in Table 10.2.

For homicide, 29 nations were consistent with the hypothesis while 11 were not ($X^2 = 8.10$, df = 1,$p < .01$). For suicide, only 17 nations were consistent with the hypothesis while 27 were not ($X^2 = 2.27$, not significant). Thus, as before, Verkko's hypothesis was confirmed for homicide rates but not for suicide rates.

Regional Differences

In 1980 the male homicide rate exceeded the female homicide rate in 96 percent of the nations in the sample. Lester (1986) reported that the male/female homicide rate ratio was highest in the Asian and American regions. For the present sample of nations in 1980, the male/female homicide rate ratio was highest in nations in Central and South America (mean 7.98), next in Asia (mean 4.31) and lowest in Europe (mean 2.09). The 1980 data confirm the results of the earlier report.

In 1980, the male suicide rate exceeded the female suicide rate in 98 percent of the nations in the sample. Fusé (1980) and Lester (1982) have both reported regional differences in the male/female suicide rate ratio in which Asian nations were found to have smaller ratios. For the 1980 suicide male/female rate ratios, the ratio was highest in Central and South America (mean 3.95), next in Europe (mean 2.55) and lowest in Asia (mean 1.43), again confirming the earlier reports.

Relationships Between the Male/Female Rate Ratios and Rates of Personal Violence

Lester (1974) reported that the male/female homicide rate ratio was associated positively with homicide rates and negatively with suicides rates in a sample of industrialized nations. To explore this, data from the fifty nations with data available for 1980 were inter-correlated.

Table 10.3

Correlations Betwen Male And Female Rates Of Personal Violence
In Fifty One Nations

	suicide rates				homicide rates			
	total	male	female	male/female	total	male	female	male/female
suicide rates:								
total	-							
male	0.99*	-						
female	0.96*	0.92*	-					
ratio	-0.20	-0.13	-0.35*	-				
homicide rates:								
total	-0.28*	-0.27	-0.29*	0.57*	-			
male	-0.29*	-0.28*	-0.30*	0.57*	1.00*	-		
female	-0.18	-0.17	-0.21	0.51*	0.95*	0.94*	-	
ratio	-0.47*	-0.46*	-0.47*	0.45*	0.68*	0.69*	0.55*	-

* statistically significant at the 5% level or better (one-tailed)

The resulting correlation matrix, shown in Table 10.3, shows that the male and female homicide rates are strongly associated (r = 0.94) as are the male and female suicide rates (r = 0.92). Homicide and suicide rates are, however, negatively associated.

The male/female homicide rate ratio was positively associated with homicide rates and negatively with suicide rates as Lester (1974) reported. The male/female suicide rate ratio was positively associated with homicide rates and not significantly associated with suicide rates.

Correlates of Male and Female Rates

The total, male and female suicide rates were correlated with all of the social characteristics in the data set. In general, the significant correlates were the same for all three rates. For example, the strongest eight correlates were the same for all three suicide rates: fertility, female labor force participation, birth rates, the employment ratio, the dependency ratio, the population growth rate, the percentage of the population under 15 years of age and the percentage over 65 years of age.

The correlates of the male/female suicide rate ratio were interesting. Where the correlates were the same as those for the total suicide rate, the sign was reversed. The male/female suicide rate ratio was negatively corrleated with the quality of life whereas the total suicide rate was positively correlated with the quality of life. Other variables similar to this included negative correlations between the male/female suicide rate ratio and the employment ratio and the caloric intake, and positive correlations with fertility, birth rates, illegitimacy rates and the percentage of the population in agriculture.

However, the male/female suicide rate ratio had a number of correlates not found for the total suicide rate: positive correlations with the percentage of Christians and of Roman Catholics and with weight and negative correlations with the gross national product growth rate and ectomorphy. Thus, the male suicide rate was relatively larger as compared to the female suicide rate in nations with higher birth and illegitimacy rates, with a greater percentage of Christians and Roman Catholics, and lower employment ratios, caloric intake, quality of life and gross national product growth rates.

In contrast, the major correlates of the male/female homicide rate ratio were similar to those for the total, male and female homicide rates. For example, the strongest correlates of the male/female homicide rate ratio were fertility, birth and illegitimacy rates, the dependency ratio, the percentage of those under the age of 15, and the percentage in agriculture (positively) and the percentage of those over the age of 65, the caloric intake and male labor force participation (negatively).

However, the male/female homicide rate ratio did have some unique correlates: urban population growth (positively), and female labor force participation, the divorce rate, the military participation rate, per capita defense expenditures, literacy, political freedom, and civil rights (negatively). Thus, males were murdered at a relatively rate as compared to females in underdeveloped nations with a strong military.

FEMALE EQUALITY

In almost all nations of the world, women are killed by others at a lower rate than are men. For example in a sample of 49 nations in 1969-1971, the mean female homicide rate was 1.4 per 100,000 per year (SD = 1.0) while the mean male homicide rate was 7.9 (SD = 11.1). However, since male and female homicide rates were strongly associated (Pearson $r = 0.81$, $n = 49$, two-tailed $p < .001$), the social predictors of female homicide rates are very similar to the social predictors of male homicide rates.

Stewart and Winter (1977) derived two measures for female equality for nations of the world using data from the later 1960s and the early 1970s. They factor-analyzed a large number of socio-economic variables and derived two factor scores for the nations, one measuring social-educational equality and one measuring economic equality. The measures are given in Stewart and Winter (1977, p. 546). The present data set was examined for the degree to which measures of suicide and homicide by gender were associated with Stewart and Winter's indices.

Correlations between Stewart and Winter's indices of equality and the 1970 rates of suicide and homicide by gender are shown in Table 10.4. It can be seen that suicide rates, for both men and women, were higher where there was more gender equality in both education and economics. Where economic equality was greater, the female/male suicide rate ratio was also higher, meaning that the suicide rate for women was relatively higher.

Table 10.4

Indices Of Equality And Rates Of Personal Violence

	social-educational equality	economic equality	
total suicide rate	0.47*	0.45*	(n's = 45-51)
male suicide rate	0.33*	0.45*	
female suicide rate	0.32*	0.45*	
female/male suicide rate	-0.15	0.29*	
total homicide rate	-0.07	-0.05	(n's = 40-43)
male homicide rate	-0.12	-0.07	
female homicide rate	0.07	0.12	
female/male homicide rate	0.02	0.17	

* two-tailed p < .05 or better

Homicide rates were not associated with the measures of gender equality. The correlation of the female/male homicide rate ratio with the measure of social-education equality was 0.02 and with the measure of economic equality was 0.17. After controls for the gross national product per capita, the partial correlations were -0.54 (p < .001) and 0.12 respectively. Thus, the results indicate that, as the social and education conditions for women become more equal to those of men in a nation, the female/male homicide rate ratio is *lower*, that is, in the more egalitarian nations, women are murdered relatively less often. This is in opposition to the hypothesis which guided the study which predicted that social equality might result in equality in the risk of being murdered. This result was, however, contingent upon the economic level of the nation being controlled for in the statistical analysis.

GENDER DIFFERENCES IN METHOD

Lester (1993, 1994) noted that the suicide rate for men was consistently higher than that for women in almost all nations, and he wondered whether this sex difference was found for each method for suicide. Data were available for 25 nations for 1980[8], and the results are shown in Table 10.5.

Table 10.5

Gender Differences In Suicide Rates By Each Method, 25 nations, 1980

	men	women	t_{24}
all methods	21.1	9.1	6.65*
solids/liquids	3.0	3.1	0.90
domestic gas	0.2	0.1	2.38*
other gas	1.5	0.2	5.11*
hanging, etc	8.6	2.5	4.66*
submersion	1.1	1.3	2.06*
firearms, etc	4.1	0.4	5.40*
cutting, etc	0.4	0.1	6.25*
jumping	1.0	0.8	3.47*
other	1.1	0.6	5.83*

* significant two-tailed p < .05 or better

It can be seen that the suicide rates for men and women by solid and liquid substances did not differ significantly. However, men had much higher suicide rates by the violent methods of firearms and hanging. Lester (1993) suggested that the higher use of violent methods for suicide by men may be a result of testosterone, a hormone known to be associated with aggressive behavior.

DISCUSSION

Our results indicate that homicide rates and suicide rates are higher for males than for females in general. The male/female rate ratio for homicide is lower in European nations, whereas the male/female rate ratio for suicide is lower in Asia.

Verkko's hypothesis that the size of and changes in the homicide rate is caused mainly by the male homicide rate was supported. No such effects were found for suicide rates. Finally, the gender difference in national sui-

8 Australia, Austria, Belgium, Brazil, Canada, Denmark, England & Wales, Finland, France, Hungary, Ireland, Israel, Italy, Japan, the Netherlands, New Zealand, Norway, Scotland, South Africa, Spain, Sweden, Switzerland, Turkey, the USA and West Germany.

cide rates was shown to be primarily a result of the higher suicide rate in men by violent methods (such as firearms and hanging).

It will be of interest to see whether suicide and homicide rates will continue to show these trends in future decades.

REFERENCES

Fusé, T. To be or not to be. *Stress,* 1980, 1(3), 18-25.

Lester, D. Sex differences in the homicide rate. *Psychological Reports,* 1973, 33, 250.

Lester, D. A cross-national study of suicide and homicide. *Behavior Science Research,* 1974, 9, 307-318.

Lester, D. The distribution of sex and age among completed suicides. *International Journal of Social Psychiatry,* 1982, 28, 256-260.

Lester, D. The distribution of sex and age among victims of homicide. *International Journal of Social Psychiatry,* 1986, 32(2), 47-50.

Lester, D. Testosterone and suicide. *Personality & Individual Differences,* 1993, 15, 347-348.

Lester, D. Sex differences in methods for suicide. *Perceptual & Motor Skills,* 1994, 79, 418.

Stewart, A. J., & Winter, D. G. (1977). The nature and causes of female suppression. *Signs,* 2, 531-553.

Verkko, V. *Homicide and suicide in Finland.* Copenhagen: C.E.S. Gads Verlag, 1951.

Chapter 11

Trends in Suicide and Homicide from 1970 to 1984

Epidemiologists often note changes in suicide and homicide rates in their own nation over time. For example, Huchcroft and Tanney (1989) reported that, in Canada from 1971 to 1985, the suicide rate for men rose while the suicide rate for women declined. The male/female suicide rate ratio, therefore, increased. They suggested that sociologists could profitably examine the social changes that might account for these different changes in the suicidal behavior of men and women.

An important question is whether the changes in the suicide rates of men and women in one country are typical of other nations of the world. The present analysis sought to examine comparable data for all available nations of the world.

Changes in the Suicide and Homicide Rates Over Time [9]

The suicide and homicide rates, overall and for men and women separately, were obtained from the *Statistics Annual*, which is published annually by the World Health Organization. The period chosen was 1970 to

9 This section is based on Lester (1990).

1984 since this was the fifteen year period for which the largest sample of nations (with populations over one million in 1980) could be obtained.

Each set of rates was subjected to a simple linear regression over the fifteen year period, and the slope (b) calculated.

The results of the regressions for suicide rates for the 23 nations are shown in Table 11.1. An increase in the male rate and a decrease in the female rate (and, therefore, an increase in the male/female rate ratio) was observed for Australia, Canada, Chile, England and Wales, Germany (FDR), Japan and the USA.

Table 11.1

Results Of The Linear Regressions Over Time (1970-1984) For 23 Nations: Data Shown Are The b Coefficients Using Rates Per Million

Nation	Suicide Rate			Homicide Rate		
	men	women	men/women	men	women	men/women
Australia	0.22	-2.34*	0.14*	0.17	0.12	-0.31
Austria	6.42*	0.62	3.34*	-3.57	0.21*	-2.45*
Bulgaria	4.24*	1.06*	2.17*	0.50	0.51	-7.78
Canada	4.62*	-0.11	7.50	0.17	-0.07	2.17
Chile	0,51	-0.42*	14.07*	-1.17	-0.02	-11.81*
Denmark	6.92*	3.39*	0.49	0.48*	0.21	3.35
England & Wales	2.01*	-0.35	4.24*	-0.17	-0.09	-0.96
Finland	2.95*	0.29	1.89	0.10	0.25	-4.53
France	7.39*	2.96*	-0.25	0.40*	0.29*	-1.69
Germany (FDR)	1.48*	-0.77*	2.14*	-0.30*	0.09*	-4.06*
Greece	0.81*	0.16	1.86	0.30*	0.19*	-3.56
Hungary	11.63*	5.24*	-0.56	0.54*	0.29*	0.15
Ireland	5.16*	2.41*	-10.51	0.53	0.16	9.24
Israel	-0.17	-1.67*	5.16*	0.96*	0.24	3.64
Japan	6.11*	-0.92	5.62*	-0.51*	-0.19*	-2.71
Netherlands	3.45*	2.05*	0.37	0.39*	0.19*	0.32
New Zealand	4.19*	1.07	7.23*	0.48	0.14	3.07
Norway	7.14*	2.52*	-2.86	0.61*	0.33	0.65
Portugal	0.29	1.43*	-9.86*	0.80	0.12	7.65
Scotland	4.24*	0.17	6.26*	0.18	0.38*	-4.67
Sweden	-2.30*	-0.75	-0.46	0.36*	0.06	3.07
Switzerland	7.62*	3.26*	-0.43	0.31	0.24	-0.46
USA	1.77*	-1.08*	8.32*	-0.25	0.23	-3.00*

* statistically signifcant at the 5% level or better

Eight nations, on the other hand, showed a pattern of increasing male suicide rates, increasing female rates and an increasing male/female rate ratio (Austria, Bulgaria, Denmark, Finland, Greece, the Netherlands, New Zealand, and Scotland), which appears, therefore, to be mainly a European phenomenon. Another common pattern (increasing male and female rates, but a decreasing male/female rate ratio) was found in six European nations (France, Hungary, Ireland, Norway, Portugal, and Switzerland).

The most common pattern for homicide rates was increasing male and female rates and an increasing male/female rate ratio (nine nations), followed by increaaing male and female rates and a decreasing male/female rate ratio (seven nations).

The present results indicate, therefore, that there is a diversity in the patterns of changing suicide and homicide rates. The next study was designed to examine the reasons for differences in the patterns of change in the different nations.

CORRELATES OF THE CHANGING SUICIDE AND HOMICIDE RATES

Javanainen (1989) argued that, as the life styles of men and women become more similar, their suicide rates should converge. He demonstrated that the male/female ratio for suicide rates was smaller among professional workers and the more educated, for example, and argued that these are the groups for whom the life styles of women are closer to those of men. Thus, it might be expected that nations in which women have more equality with men would have declining male/female mortality ratios as compared to nations in which women have less equality. The present analysis examined this hypothesis.

Data were available for the suicide and homicide rates by sex for 22 nations of the world for 1970 to 1984 from the *Statistics Annual* published annually by the World Health Organization (the same sample as in Table 11.1 but excluding Scotland for which social indicators were not available).

A number of social variables from 1970 were examined for their ability to predict changes in the male/female mortality ratios. Of most importance were measures of social-educational equality and economic equality derived by Stewart and Winter (1977) for the period 1965-1970. These measures were supplemented by the gross domestic product per capita from Summers and Heston (1984), alcohol consumption per capita from Adrian (1984), and divorce rates, birth rates, and the percentage of residents over the age of 65 from the World Bank (1984), variables which have been shown in previous research to be associated with suicide and homicide rates (Lester, 1988).

As can be seen in Table 11.2, changes in the male/female suicide rate ratio was associated only with the percentage of elderly (Pearson r = -0.53, two-tailed p < .01). Thus, in nations with a greater proportion of elderly, the male/female suicide rate ratio was more likely to decline subsequently. Measures of sexual equality were not related to the male/female suicide rate ratio.

Table 11.2

Correlations Of Social Variables With Changes In The Male/Female Mortality Ratios

	male/female suicide rates	male/female homicide rates
socio-education equality	0.27	0.06
economic equality	0.23	-0.48*
domestic product/capita	0.22	0.06
alcohol consumption	-0.10	-0.14
birth rate	0.33	0.01
proportion of elderly	-0.53**	0.22
divorce rate	0.24	-0.14
suicide rate	-0.02	-0.15
homicide rate	0.49*	-0.27

* statistically significant at the 5% level or better.

The male/female homicide rate ratio was significantly associated with the measure of economic equality (r = -0.48, p < .05). The male/female homicide rate ratio was more likely to decline in nations with greater female economic equality.

In backward multiple regressions, however, economic equality had a positive effect on the male/female suicide rate ratio (beta = 0.54, p < .01) and a negative effect on the male/female homicide rate ratio (beta = -0.48, p < .05).

Interestingly, changes in the male/female ratios for suicide rates and for homicide rates were negatively associated (r = -0.64, p < .01). When one ratio declined, the other ratio tended to increase.

Discussion

The present study found (at least in the multiple regression analyses) that nations with more gender equality tended to experience an increasing male/female suicide rate ratio in subsequent years. The proportion of elderly in the nation, however, was the strongest correlate of the changing male/female suicide rate ratio.

Gender economic equality was associated with a decreasing male/female homicide rate ratio. Where women had greater economic equality with men, their risk of being murdered became more similar to that for men. The differences bewteen these results for suicide and for homicide are diffcult to account for and call for further research.

It was surprising that few of the social variables included in this study predicted trends in the male/female mortality ratios (or indeed trends in the absolute values of the male and female suicide and homicide rates). Although social variables have proven useful in associations with *concurrent* suicide and homicide rates (Lester, 1988), they seem to be less successful in *predicting* future trends in these rates.

References

Adrian, M. International trends in alcohol production, trade and consumption, and their relationship to alcohol-related problems, 1970 to 1977. *Journal of Public Health Policy*, 1984, 5, 344-367.

Huchcroft, S. A., & Tanney, B. L. Sex-specific suicide trends in suicide method, Canada, 1971-1985. *Canadian Journal of Public Health*, 1989, 80, 120-123.

Javanainen, M. Convergence of life-styles and sex ratio in suicide mortality in Finland. *Helsingin Yliopiston Sosiologian Laitos Tyoselostuksia*, 1989, No. 46, 1-19.

Lester, D. A regional analysis of suicide and homcide rates in the USA. *Social Psychiatry & Psychiatric Epidemiology*, 1988, 23, 202-205.

Lester, D. Changes to suicide rates unique to Canada? *Canadian Journal of Public Health*, 1990, 81, 240-241.

Stewart, A. J., & Winter, D. G. The nature and causes of female suppression. *Signs*, 1977, 2, 531-553.

Summers, R., & Heston, A. Improved international comparisons of real product and its composition. *Review of Income & Wealth*, 1984, 30, 207-262.

World Bank. *World Tables*. Baltimore: Johns Hopkins University Press, 1984.

CHAPTER 12

A CRITICAL-MASS THEORY OF SUICIDE AND HOMICIDE RATES

There have been a variety of approaches to exploring whether suggestion plays a role in the precipitation of suicidal behavior. Phillips' research on the effects of newspaper and television publicity (e.g., Phillips, 1974) shows convincingly that suicides do increase in the days after a publicized suicide by a famous person. In addition, other investigators have studied the effects of newspaper strikes (Motto, 1970), documented epidemics of suicidal behavior (Hankoff, 1979), suicide pacts (Ohara and Reynolds, 1970), and the temporal clustering of suicides jumping off the Golden Gate Bridge (Kirch and Lester, 1986).

Another approach to documenting suggestion effects is suggested by the writing of Schelling (1978), an economist. Schelling has noted that people's behavior often depends upon how many other people are behaving in the same way. An activity becomes self-sustaining (and may increase in incidence) once the frequency of that activity increases beyond a certain level. If this idea is applied to national suicide rates, it can be hypothesized that a given suicide rate creates a certain amount of publicity about suicide and a particular likelihood that a person in the society knows someone who has committed suicide. Once the suicide rate reaches a critical level, the publicity and probability of knowing suicides increase to such an extent that the effect of suggestion (or imitation) makes the behavior self-sustaining and perhaps accelerates it.

Table 12.1

Suicide And Homicide Rates In 1970 And The Change In The Rates By 1980

	suicide			homicide		
	1970 rate	% change	absolute change	1970 rate	% change	absolute change
Argentina	10.0	-28	-2.8	7.3	-49	-3.6
Australia	12.7	-11	-1.4	1.5	27	0.4
Austria	23.1	13	2.9	1.3	0	0
Belgium	15.7	37	5.8	1.0	60	0.6
Bulgaria	11.2	24	2.7	2.6	4	0.1
Canada	11.4	24	2.7	2.0	15	0.3
Chile	6.2	-11	-0.7	3.9	-31	-1.2
Colombia	2.7	30	0.8	14.1	165	23.3
Costa Rica	2.8	57	1.6	3.9	21	0.8
Czechoslov	24.2	18	-4.4	1.4	-21	-0.3
Denmark	22.4	30	6.7	0.8	50	0.4
Dominican R	2.5	-20	-0.5	-	-	-
Ecuador	2.3	22	0.5	7.2	-17	-1.2
El Salvador	7.7	57	4.4	19.5	354	69.1
Finland	22.1	12	2.6	2.4	21	0.5
France	15.5	24	3.7	0.8	25	0.2
Germany W	21.0	2	0.4	1.3	-8	-0.1
Greece	3.3	-3	-0.1	0.6	17	0.1
Guatemala	3.2	-69	-2.2	20.2	219	44.2
Hong Kong	10.6	17	1.8	1.5	0	0
Hungary	34.7	30	10.3	2.1	19	0.4
India	8.3	-28	-2.3	2.9	10	0.3
Ireland	2.1	195	4.1	0.4	200	0.8
Israel	6.6	-9	-0.6	6.2	-71	-4.4
Italy	5.7	25	1.4	0.9	100	0.9
Japan	15.1	16	2.4	1.3	-23	-0.3
Jordan	0.7	214	1.5	-	-	-
Kuwait	0.3	133	0.4	-	-	-
Mexico	0.8	112	0.9	14.1	24	3.4
Netherlands	7.9	29	2.3	0.5	60	0.3
New Zealand	9.3	10	0.9	1.1	27	0.3
Norway	8.2	51	4.2	0.6	83	0.5
Panama	3.2	-37	-1.2	3.5	-34	-1.2
Paraguay	1.5	0	0	6.6	-18	-1.2
Peru	1.9	-37	-0.7	1.7	-41	-0.7
Poland	11.4	11	1.3	1.1	-9	-0.1
Portugal	8.0	4	0.3	0.9	56	0.5
Puerto Rico	9.7	-12	-1.2	12.4	18	2.2
Singapore	9.7	1	0.1	1.8	6	0.1
Spain	4.3	2	0.1	0.3	233	0.7
Sri Lanka	19.0	14	8.8	-	-	-
Sweden	21.5	-11	-2.4	0.9	44	0.4
Switzerland	18.2	36	6.5	0.6	67	0.4
Syria	0.6	-33	-0.2	-	-	-
Taiwan	12.1	-18	-2.2	-	-	-
Thailand	3.9	82	3.2	-	-	-
Trinidad	6.6	-27	-1.8	3.9	-15	-0.6
UK	8.1	6	0.5	0.8	25	0.2
USA	11.4	5	0.6	8.3	23	1.9
Venezuela	6.8	-31	-2.1	7.9	-42	-3.3
Yugoslavia	13.7	8	1.1	3.4	-38	-1.3
Zimbabwe	6.0	2	0.1	-	-	-

Lester (1987) conducted a preliminary test of this idea by studying thirty three nations in 1970 and 1980. The absolute increase (but not the percentage increase) in the suicide rate during the 1970s for these nations was associated with the suicide rate in 1970. Nations with the higher suicide rates in 1970 experienced greater increases in the suicide rate by 1980.

Lester (1988a) replicated this study showing that the effect was present after two years and as strong after seven years as at the end of the decade. Further analyses showed that this critical-mass hypothesis was shown more clearly in the nations in the sample with above average suicide rates (defined as above the median suicide rate of the sample of nations).

Data on the suicide rates in 1970 and 1980 were available for fifty-two nations and are shown in Table 12.1. The correlation between the 1970 suicide rates and the absolute change by 1980 was 0.42 (one-tailed $p < .01$), but between the 1970 suicide rates and the percentage change by 1980 -0.18 (not significant), just as Lester (1987) found.

HOMICIDE

Lester (1989b) explored whether the critical mass hypothesis applied to homicide and, for a small sample of seventeen nations, confirmed that indeed nations with the higher homicide rates in 1970 had a larger absolute increase by 1980. For the present data set, rates were available for forty five nations, and the correlation between 1970 homicide rates and the absolute change by 1980 was 0.71 (two-tailed $p < .001$) while the correlation between 1970 homicide rates and the percentage change by 1980 was 0.38 (two-tailed $p < .01$). Thus, the critical mass hypothesis appears to apply also to homicide rates.

Reported suicide rates to the World Health Organization (annual) now extend into the following decade, permitting an examination of epidemiological trends for the 1980s. An analysis of these rates shows that the trends in the 1980s are very different from the 1970s. Data were available for 25 nations for 1970, 1980, and 1990. Data for a further ten nations were available for 1969, 1979 and 1989 (see Table 12.2).

Table 12.2

Suicide Rates In Nations Of The World In The Last Two Decades

	1970	1980	1990
Austria	24.2	25.7	23.6
Bulgaria	11.9	13.6	14.7
Canada	11.3	14.0	12.7
Czechoslovakia	25.2	20.0	17.9
Denmark	21.5	31.6	24.1
England/Wales	8.0	8.8	7.8
Finland	21.3	25.7	30.3
France	15.4	19.4	20.1
Greece	3.2	3.3	3.5
Hungary	34.8	44.9	39.9
Ireland	1.8	6.3	9.5
Japan	15.2	17.6	16.4
Mexico	1.1	1.4	2.3
Netherlands	8.1	10.1	9.7
N. Ireland	3.9	5.2	9.9
Norway	8.4	12.4	15.5
Poland	11.2	10.7	13.0
Portgual	7.5	7.4	8.8
Puerto Rico	9.2	9.1	10.5
Scotland	7.6	10.0	10.5
Singapore	8.9	11.2	13.1
Switzerland	18.6	25.7	21.9
USSR	22.7	26.9	21.1
West Germany	21.3	20.9	17.5
Yugoslavia	13.5	14.7	15.3
	1969	1979	1989
Argentina	10.2	6.7	7.1
Chile	6.8	5.9	5.6
Costa Rica	3.1	3.4	5.8
Hong Kong	8.6	13.5	10.5
Israel	7.1	6.6	7.8
Italy	5.4	7.0	7.5
New Zealand	10.0	9.7	13.9
Spain	4.4	4.1	7.7
Sweden	22.0	20.5	18.6
USA	11.1	12.1	12.2

Although the suicide rate for the 35 nations rose from 12.13 to 13.89 from 1970 to 1980 ($t_{34} = 3.28$, two-tailed $p < .01$), there was no significant change from 1980 to 1990 ($t_{34} = 0.01$; means 13.89 and 13.89 respectively).

Furthermore, while the nations with *higher* suicide rates in 1970 experienced a greater increase in absolute suicide rates by 1980 (Pearson $r = 0.34$), the nations with *lower* suicide in 1980 experienced a greater absolute increase in suicide rates by 1990 ($r = -0.67$).

This can be seen quite dramatically in Table 12.2. From 1970 to 1980, Denmark and Hungary had the greatest abolsute increases in suicide rates, and they had high suicide rates in 1970. In contrast, Northern Ireland, New Zealand and Finland had the greatest absolute increases in suicide rates from 1980 to 1990, and two of these nations (Northern Ireland and New Zealand) had relatively low suicide rates in 1980. Hungary and Denmark both experienced large *decreases* in their suicide rates from 1980 to 1990.

These results suggest (1) the critical mass theory of suicide no longer applied in the 1980s, (2) that suicide prevention efforts may have operated successfully in the 1980s, or (3) that research is needed to explore whether the increase in suicide rates in nations in the 1980s with low suicide rates is a reflection of greater accuracy in reporting suicides or due to social trends in those nations.

DISCUSSION

Lester (1988a, 1988b) showed shown that the critical-mass theory explains the changing suicide rates of nations of the world during the 1970s. It is important, however, to ask whether that sample at that time was deviant and whether the theory will apply at other times.

Lester (1989a) repeated the study using the period of 1960 to 1970 and replicated the results found for the 1970s though the effect was no longer statistically significant. Furthermore, data from the 1980s examined in the present study failed to confirm the results from the 1970s.[10]

---

10 Lester (1988b) argued that the hypothesis would not be confirmed if the states of the USA were used since the publicity attending suicide would not be restricted to within a single state and since residential mobility is high. He failed to find the critical-mass effect for the forty eight continental states from 1970 to 1980.

Thus, the validity of the critical-mass theory is questionable, and it will be of interest to explore whether data from the 1990s support the theory. The implication of the theory is, of course, that suicide rates of nations with high enough suicide rates will continue to increase unless effective suicide prevention techniques are introduced into the society. Without such suicide prevention efforts, suicide rates will continue to rise, and the critical-mass theory does not predict that they should ever level off. Explanation of any levelling off would require different theoretical concepts.

REFERENCES

Hankoff, L. The armed forces. In L. Hankoff & B. Einsidler (Eds.) *Suicide.* Littleton, MA: PSG, 1979, 343-349.

Kirch, M. R., & Lester, D. Suicides from the Golden Gate Bridge. *Psychological Reports*, 1986, 59, 13.

Lester, D. Indirect evidence for effects of suggestion in suicide. *Psychological Reports*, 1987, 61, 576.

Lester, D. A critical-mass theory of national suicide rates. *Suicide & Life-Threatening Behavior*, 1988a, 18, 279-284.

Lester, D. The critical mass hypothesis of suicide: a test in the United States of America. *Psychological Reports*, 1988b, 62, 626.

Lester, D. The critical mass hypothesis applied to national suicide rates: a replication in the 1960s. *Psychological Reports*, 1989a, 64, 746.

Lester, D. The critical mass hypothesis and homicide. *Psychological Reports*, 1989b, 64, 146.

Motto, J. Newspaper influence on suicide. *Archives of General Psychiatry*, 1970, 23, 143-148.

Ohara, K., & Reynolds, D. Love-pact suicides. *Omega*, 1970, 1, 159-166.

Phillips, D. P. The influence of suggestion on suicide. *American Sociological Review*, 1974, 39, 340-354.

Schelling, T. C. *Micromotives and macrobehavior*. New York: Norton, 1978.

CHAPTER 13

SUICIDE AND HOMICIDE ACROSS THE LIFESPAN

The most striking epidemiological feature of suicide rates in America is the increasing male suicide rate with age whereas the female suicide rate peaks at age 45-54, but this pattern is not found in every nation. Fusé (1980) described three patterns for the variation of suicide rates with age. The Hungarian pattern is one in which the suicide rate increases regularly with age. The Japanese pattern is one with two peaks, a lesser peak in young adulthood and a major peak in old age. The Scandinavian pattern is one which peaks in middle age and is an inverted U-shaped curve.

Lester (1982) examined the validity of Fusé's hypothesis for suicide rates of nations of the world in 1975. The patterns Lester identified are shown in Table 13.1. Lester concluded that Fusé's patterns were useful for describing the variation of suicide rates with age, but that his labels for them were not the best since, for example, Japanese males had the Hungarian pattern rather than the Japanese pattern. Furthermore, not all patterns could be fitted to one of the three proposed by Fusé. (For example, Danish and Swedish males fell into none of the three patterns.)

Lester also divided the nations into four groups on the basis of their gross national product per capita. In general, male suicide rates increased with age for all four groups of nations, and men aged 75 and older had the highest suicide rates (see Table 13.2). For females, the peak age for

Table 13.1

Patterns Of Suicide In Men And Women (from Lester [1982])

	males	females
Hungarian (peak in old age)		
	Austria	Austria
	Bulgaria	Czechoslovakia
	Chile	Germany
	Cuba	Hungary
	Czechoslovakia	Italy
	England & Wales	Singapore
	France	West Germany
	Hong Kong	
	Italy	
	Japan	
	Portugal	
	Spain	
	West Germany	
Scandinavian (peak for age 45-54 or 55-64)		
	Canada	Australia
	Norway	Canada
	Poland	Denmark
		Netherlands
		Poland
		Sweden
		USA
Japanese (minor peak for age 15-24, 25-34 or 35-44)		
	Belgium	Bulgaria
	Greece	Hong Kong
	Puerto Rico	Japan
	Singapore	Portugal
	Uruguay	Spain
	Venezuela	
	USA	

Table 13.2

The Age Distribution Of Suicide Rates In Males And Females For Nations Wtih Differing GNP/Capita, Ranked From Highest (1) To Lowest (8)

		5-14	15-24	25-34	35-44	45-54	55-64	65-74	75+
Males									
gnp/capita:	top quartile	8	7	6	5	3.5	3.5	2	1
	second quartile	8	7	6	5	4	3	2	1
	third quartile	8	7	6	5	4	3	2	1
	fourth quartile	8	7	6	4	5	3	2	1
Females									
gnp/capita:	top quartile	8	7	6	4	2	1	3	5
	second quartile	8	7	6	5	3.5	2	1	3.5
	third quartile	8	7	6	5	4	3	2	1
	fourth quartile	8	1	5	7	6	4	2.5	2.5

suicide rose (from the age group 55-64 to 65-74 and then 75+) with decreasing gross national product per capita from the first to the third quartile and then dropped dramatically to the 15-24 year old group for the poorest nations (those in the fourth quartile).

The suicide rates by age for nations of the world with populations greater than one million who have reported suicide rates to the World Health Organization for 1970, 1980 and 1988 are shown in Table 13.3. Several patterns are clear.

(1) Monotonically Increasing

Several nations had suicide rates in 1980 which rose with age for both sexes: Austria, Bulgaria, France, Greece, Hong Kong, Hungary, Italy, Japan, Portugal, Singapore and Spain. This is a diverse group of nations, European and Asian, relatively rich and relatively poor.

In some of these nations, the peak in old age is striking. For example, in Hungary the suicide rate for men aged 75+ in 1980 was 202.2 per 100,000 per year compared to 31.5 for men aged 15-24. The rate for the elderly men was double that found in Austria, Bulgaria and France, the nations with the next highest suicides for elderly men.

Table 13.3

Suicide Rates By Age In Countries Of The World In 1970, 1980 And 1988

	Age						
	15-24	25-34	35-44	45-54	55-64	65-74	75+
Australia							
1970 male	12.4	20.1	26.1	33.6	30.9	31.9	38.5
1980 male	17.6	22.9	23.4	22.3	24.0	22.4	31.9
1988 male	27.8	28.2	26.0	24.4	23.8	27.7	39.8
1970 female	4.7	7.8	11.8	14.6	17.0	14.4	9.5
1980 female	4.5	6.9	9.8	9.2	7.9	7.1	9.1
1988 female	4.5	7.2	7.5	8.2	8.7	7.4	10.0
Austria							
1970 male	27.0	31.7	46.6	58.5	64.6	72.7	77.7
1980 male	28.8	36.3	43.9	59.3	56.3	72.6	85.7
1988 male	27.2	38.6	42.2	48.1	47.6	58.6	107.5
1970 female	5.7	8.2	16.4	22.3	25.7	27.6	29.4
1980 female	6.7	11.1	14.3	20.7	23.0	29.1	33.9
1988 female	4.7	10.3	13.6	16.5	22.5	22.9	29.7
Bulgaria							
1970 male	9.0	11.6	11.3	19.3	27.1	53.2	108.3
1980 male	11.1	12.9	16.3	21.9	26.8	52.2	108.7
1988 male	12.5	15.7	21.8	25.6	33.7	51.2	118.1
1970 female	4.8	4.9	5.3	9.8	15.9	18.4	34.5
1980 female	7.4	5.8	5.7	8.2	14.4	17.0	31.9
1988 female	6.2	6.3	4.1	9.5	14.3	21.6	42.3
Canada							
1970 male	15.6	20.1	26.6	27.9	31.9	28.0	24.6
1980 male	24.8	29.5	25.1	30.7	28.5	26.9	38.1
1988 male	26.9	29.2	26.1	24.2	28.0	26.2	30.6
1970 female	4.8	8.6	10.6	14.5	11.4	9.5	4.6
1980 female	5.4	8.1	8.8	13.7	12.1	9.5	5.9
1988 female	4.9	7.1	9.8	9.9	6.9	6.1	6.2
Denmark							
1970 male	11.1	25.4	39.5	55.9	48.8	45.7	55.0
1980 male	16.3	42.7	61.8	70.7	71.8	60.4	81.3
1988 male	15.9	33.6	44.7	50.5	52.6	47.2	69.2
1970 female	5.7	10.6	22.6	30.2	34.1	26.7	19.1

1980 female	7.7	16.7	35.8	42.8	39.3	32.9	31.6
1988 female	5.5	12.0	20.6	33.2	33.2	36.0	33.1
Finland							
1970 male	22.5	41.5	55.8	60.9	62.6	66.5	50.5
1980 male	37.5	55.7	55.0	60.3	54.9	62.1	60.1
1988 male	39.6	60.4	65.8	64.4	54.7	60.3	65.6
1970 female	6.7	9.4	11.2	20.6	15.9	12.2	7.4
1980 female	9.1	9.5	11.4	16.8	16.2	22.8	9.7
1988 female	7.5	7.7	13.2	25.4	18.3	16.9	14.4
France							
1970 male	9.4	17.1	25.5	36.2	51.1	55.3	74.4
1980 male	15.7	27.4	32.7	39.7	41.2	57.1	99.6
1988 male	13.9	32.5	38.2	40.0	41.2	47.5	109.0
1970 female	4.4	7.4	8.0	11.3	16.3	17.9	18.6
1980 female	5.4	9.6	13.2	14.9	17.2	22.6	24.4
1988 female	4.2	9.0	12.7	19.8	17.6	22.9	25.3
Greece							
1970 male	1.7	3.9	6.1	6.7	10.6	10.7	11.6
1980 male	3.0	5.4	5.6	5.2	5.4	10.1	16.6
1988 male	4.8	7.4	5.7	5.9	9.9	7.5	17.5
1970 female	1.4	1.7	1.0	3.2	4.3	1.7	5.6
1980 female	0.6	1.1	1.9	2.8	2.9	4.5	6.1
1988 female	0.6	1.6	1.5	2.9	3.3	6.9	6.0
Hungary							
1970 male	27.8	48.6	63.6	78.4	85.1	104.9	146.4
1980 male	31.5	58.3	86.8	106.4	96.7	116.3	202.2
1988 male	21.0	57.8	79.4	99.7	84.8	96.0	172.9
1970 female	9.6	11.0	17.5	23.8	33.8	46.2	76.4
1980 female	8.0	16.4	26.7	36.2	42.2	52.9	90.6
1988 female	10.1	19.0	27.2	34.8	35.9	46.8	74.9
Italy							
1970 male	3.5	5.9	7.4	11.4	18.3	24.3	33.3
1980 male	5.3	8.3	9.1	14.0	17.3	26.5	37.4
1988 male	4.9	9.1	9.9	12.1	16.2	28.3	47.4
1970 female	2.3	2.7	3.5	5.2	7.0	7.5	7.8
1980 female	2.4	3.3	4.2	6.8	8.2	10.2	10.2
1988 female	1.4	2.7	3.6	5.7	7.3	9.7	11.1
Japan							

1970 male	14.0	20.1	17.8	20.1	32.3	50.4	82.1
1980 male	16.6	24.9	28.9	33.3	32.2	40.9	73.3
1988 male	10.4	21.9	26.6	41.2	37.8	39.2	72.2
1970 female	11.9	13.8	10.0	13.5	20.6	40.5	66.3
1980 female	8.2	11.4	12.5	15.1	17.8	35.5	60.2
1988 female	6.5	9.3	10.4	16.6	19.3	30.6	54.9
Netherlands							
1970 male	5.8	6.4	11.1	15.7	24.0	25.4	42.5
1980 male	8.3	14.9	15.1	17.1	22.3	26.1	41.1
1988 male	8.2	16.1	14.3	17.2	20.0	21.2	41.3
1970 female	2.1	5.5	7.5	11.0	12.6	14.9	17.5
1980 female	3.7	8.0	8.9	12.4	14.1	14.3	12.0
1988 female	2.4	8.3	9.3	11.2	14.0	13.1	10.7
Norway							
1970 male	5.4	15.0	17.4	19.2	24.7	19.6	13.3
1980 male	20.4	18.2	20.6	28.6	31.8	25.5	24.0
1988 male	26.6	31.4	27.5	36.8	34.4	25.4	33.7
1970 female	2.0	4.5	10.1	10.4	8.9	6.9	1.9
1980 female	3.3	9.0	6.7	14.2	12.1	9.6	4.7
1988 female	6.5	11.7	13.8	14.3	13.1	13.0	7.7
Portugal							
1970 male	5.6	6.2	17.5	14.5	27.6	43.4	72.2
1980 male	5.2	7.9	14.7	18.6	24.1	31.0	53.7
1988 male	6.4	8.7	10.7	20.0	23.2	33.4	49.2
1970 female	3.6	2.1	3.0	3.8	6.7	9.2	11.7
1980 female	4.1	5.4	3.8	4.2	5.4	5.6	11.0
1988 female	2.9	2.7	1.8	4.5	5.4	10.2	9.3
Switzerland							
1970 male	21.3	27.6	31.2	46.2	49.0	49.5	74.1
1980 male	34.2	36.5	42.2	46.1	63.4	58.9	80.7
1988 male	26.3	38.0	36.6	39.6	41.7	48.5	74.8
1970 female	4.7	10.2	8.8	19.5	19.1	21.7	16.0
1980 female	12.3	14.8	17.6	21.7	20.8	26.8	23.2
1988 female	7.1	10.0	13.7	17.5	19.7	22.2	26.4
UK: England & Wales							
1970 male	6.0	9.1	11.3	14.1	17.5	20.7	23.9
1980 male	6.4	13.0	15.5	15.4	17.9	18.2	21.6
1988 male	11.0	15.5	18.0	14.7	15.3	16.2	24.3

1970 female	2.6	4.4	7.4	10.3	12.9	15.3	9.7
1980 female	3.0	4.2	8.1	10.9	11.8	13.3	11.0
1988 female	2.5	3.8	4.9	6.4	6.8	8.0	8.4
UK: Scotland							
1970 male	5.8	8.6	15.6	13.1	24.0	12.9	21.7
1980 male	9.6	15.2	19.1	23.4	17.8	18.8	23.2
1988 male	20.5	23.9	22.5	26.6	18.8	12.9	24.1
1970 female	1.8	5.8	8.2	15.1	12.7	5.7	5.6
1980 female	3.1	7.0	9.6	14.3	14.3	10.9	8.1
1988 female	4.9	7.7	9.8	7.9	7.7	12.0	6.0
USA							
1970 male	13.5	19.6	22.2	27.8	32.8	36.5	41.8
1980 male	20.2	24.8	22.3	23.0	24.4	30.2	43.5
1988 male	21.9	25.0	22.9	21.7	25.0	33.0	57.8
1970 female	4.2	8.6	12.1	12.5	11.4	9.3	6.7
1980 female	4.3	7.0	8.4	9.4	8.4	6.5	5.4
1988 female	4.2	5.7	6.9	7.9	7.2	6.8	6.4
West Germany							
1970 male	19.6	27.0	35.1	43.2	51.6	53.9	75.2
1980 male	19.0	26.9	33.0	42.0	38.9	54.0	72.8
1988 male	15.8	22.7	24.4	33.0	35.5	41.3	77.8
1970 female	6.9	11.5	15.9	25.4	27.2	26.1	27.0
1980 female	5.6	9.9	14.0	20.4	23.6	27.1	25.9
1988 female	4.7	7.7	9.5	13.6	14.6	19.5	24.1

(2) Peak in Youth

Three nations had the peak suicide rate for women in the age range 15-24: Chile, Thailand and Venezuela. In Chile and Venezuela the male suicide rate peaked in the oldest group (75+), while in Thailand the male suicide rate peaked in those aged 45-64. These three nations are all relatively poor, and this suggests that the phenomenon of peak rates of suicide in young women is a feature of less developed nations.

(3) Peak in Middle Age

The rest of the nations had peak suicide rates in age groups which varied from decade to decade and for men and women. For example, the peak suicide rate for Australian women was in those aged 55-64 in 1970 and in those aged 35-44 in 1980. In New Zealand, the peak suicide rate for men rose from 65-74 in 1970 to 75+ in 1980, while in Scotland the peak age for men dropped from 55-64 in 1970 to 45-54 in 1980.

(4) The United States

The USA pattern in unimodal, with the peak at age 75+ for men and 45-54 for women. No other nation in the sample had exactly this pattern.

Girard (1993) classified the distributions of suicide rates by age as upward sloping, bimodal, convex and downward sloping. His classifications were incorporated into the present data set. For male suicide rates 23 were upward sloping, 19 bimodal, three convex and two downard sloping. The upward sloping and bimodal nations were compared on the social factors in the present data set. Nations with upward sloping age distributions for male suicide rates had higher suicide rates, gross domestic product per capita, quality of life, life expectancy, percentage urban, female and male labor force participation, union membership, percentage of elderly, death rates, caloric intake, height and wieght, alcohol consumption, and literacy and lower infant mortality, birth rates, illegitimacy rates, total and urban population growth, child labor, percentage of males, population per hospital bed, doctor and nurse, gnp growth and percentage of children.[11] Thus, an upward sloping distribution of male suicide rates by age seemed to be more common in the more economically developed nations, while the bimodal distribution seemed to be more common in the less economically developed nations.

The distributions of suicide rates by age for women were more evenly distrubted over the four types: nine upward sloping, 12 bimodal, 13 convex and 13 downward sloping.

The nations with upward sloping distributions for women had the highest suicide rates, percentage of elderly, female labor force participation, alcohol consumption, percentage of Roman Catholics, per capita expenditures on defense and literacy and the lowest homicide rates, illegitimate births and percentage of males. This describes the situation in nations like Austria and France.

Nations with bimodal distributions for women had the highest marriage rates and gnp growth and the lowest levels of political freedom and civil rights, such as Greece and Bulgaria.

Nations with a convex distribution for women had the highest gross domestic product per capita, quality of life, life expectancy, percentage urban, male and female labor force participation, divorce rate, urbanization, percentage of elderly, caloric intake, height, weight, political freedom, civil liberties and literacy, and the lowest levels of fertility, infant mortality, total and urban population growth, gnp growth, child labor, population per hospital bed, doctor and nurse, percentage of children and percentage of Roman Catholics. This is characteristic of such nations as Finland and New Zealand.

Finally, those nations with a downward sloping distribution for women had the highest homicide rate, birth rate, infant mortality rate, total and urban population growth, child labor, population per hospital bed, doctor, and nurse, percentage of men, and percentage of children and illegitimacy, and the lowest rates of suicide, quality of life, gross domestic product per capita, life expectancy, percentage urban, male and female labor force participation, marriage, divorce, percentage of elderly, percentage in unions,

---

11 The two groups of nations did not differ in homicide rates, population, civil liberties, political freedom, marriage, divorce, population density, area, percentage Christian, percentage Roman Catholic, percentage Muslim, inflation, unemployment, military participation rate and expenditures, corn consumption, or ectomorphy.

alcohol consumption, per capita expenditure on defense, literacy, height and weight. This is characteristic of such nations as Mexico and the Philippines.

Thus, there appear to be two distributions for women characteristic of the more develop nations (upward-sloping and convex) and two for less developed nations (bimodal and downward sloping).

Girard himself proposed (and felt that he had confirmed) four hypotheses. First, convex and upward-sloping distributions will be characteristic of developed nations. This agrees with our findings for men and women. Second, downward sloping patterns will be characteristic of less developed nations, again confirmed by our data.

In addition, Girard hypothesized that bimodal distributions will be characteristic of nations at an intermediate level of development, and that the shift from downard sloping to bimodal to upward sloping distributions occurs at a lower level of development for men than for women. The data presented earlier in this chapter (see Table 13.2) support the second of these hypotheses but not the first.

LINEAR TRENDS IN SUICIDE RATES BY AGE

A simple way of measuring linear trends in suicide rates by age is to calculate a Spearman rho correlation coefficient between the suicide rate for each age group and the age group (ranging from 14-25 to 75+) (Lester, 1993). This was possible for 36 nations for 1980, and the results are shown in Table 13.4.

The values of these Spearman rho correlation coefficients were then correlated with some of the social indicators in the data set (Table 13.5). It can be seen that a monotonicaly increasing suicide rate with age was associated with developed, urban and aging nations for both men and for women.

CHANGES IN SUICIDE RATES IN THE 1980S

In the 1970s, the striking epidemiological feature of suicide rates was the increasing rate of teenage suicide. As can be seen in Table 13.3, the

Table 13.4

Spearman Correlations Between Suicide Rates And Age

	men	women
Australia	0.61	0.39
Austria	0.96	1.00
Bulgaria	1.00	0.86
Canada	0.57	0.34
Chile	0.43	-0.10
Costa Rica	0.68	-0.83
Denmark	0.79	0.39
Ecudaor	-0.68	-0.97
England & Wales	0.96	0.86
Finland	0.61	0.61
France	1.00	1.00
Greece	0.78	1.00
Guatemala	-0.68	-0.10
Hong Kong	0.96	0.96
Hungary	0.96	1.00
Ireland	-0.11	0.11
Israel	0.82	0.96
Italy	1.00	0.99
Japan	0.96	1.00
Netherlands	1.00	0.79
New Zealand	0.64	0.46
Northern Ireland	0.21	-0.19
Norway	0.64	0.29
Paraguay	0.14	-0.21
Portugal	1.00	0.78
Scotland	0.61	0.53
Singapore	0.82	0.86
Spain	1.00	0.96
Sri Lanka	0.14	-0.50
Surinam	0.54	0.43
Sweden	0.82	0.43
Switzerland	0.96	0.93
USA	0.79	0.04
Venezuela	0.96	-0.79
West Germany	0.96	0.96
Yugoslavia	1.00	0.96

Table 13.5

Social Correlates Of Correlations Between Age And Suicide Rates

	men	women
rho for men	-	0.67
gdp/capita	0.50*	0.45*
population	0.19	0.06
% children	-0.70*	-0.77*
% elderly	0.54*	0.66*
% urban	0.44*	0.35*
birth rate	-0.73*	-0.77*
death rate	0.00	0.32
marriage rate	0.23	0.06

* two-tailed p < .05 or better

1980s have been a time of increasing suicide rates in the elderly. For Australia, Bulgaria, Finland, France, Italy, and Norway the suicide rates for those aged 75+ peaked for men and women in 1988 (the latest year for which data are available). In addition, the suicide rates for men aged 75+ peaked in 1988 in Austria, England and Wales, Greece, Scotland, the USA and West Germany, while the suicide rates for women aged 75+ peaked in 1988 in Canada, Denmark and Switzerland. Thus, suicide in the elderly may become the new focus of concern for suicidologists in the 1990s.

It is interesting to note that some countries have witnessed a decreasing elderly suicide rate since 1970 (Japan, the Netherlands and Portugal), and it would be useful if we could ascertain why these nations differ in their changing suicide rates for youth and for the elderly.

Youth Suicide Rates

Lester (1988) examined changes in the suicide rates of young people in nations of the world from 1970 to 1980 when youth suicide rates were reputed to be rising (see Table 13.6). The nations with the greatest percentage increases from 1970 to 1980 for the group aged 15-24 were Norway (+224%), Spain (+93%), Switzerland (+80%) and Thailand (+78%). In addition, New Zealand, Finland, Canada and the Netherlands experienced large increases in their youth suicide rate from 1970 to 1980.

In contrast, several nations experienced a drop in the youth suicide rate, including Guatemala (-51%), Chile (-32%) and Venezuela (-28%). West Germany and Japan also experienced decreases during this period. However, twenty-two nations witnessed an increase in the youth suicide rate during the 1970s compared to only five witnessing a decrease.

Closer examination reveals that sometimes the changing youth suicide rate parallelled the changing total suicide rate, but sometimes did not. Differences were also found for male and female youths. Using a criterion that the percentage increase in the youth suicide rate must be ten percent or greater than the percentage increase in the overall suicide rate, the following nations had a rising youth suicide rate in both males and females: Finland, the Netherlands, New Zealand, Norway, Scotland, Spain and Switzerland. Nations with a rising youth suicide rate only in males were

Table 13.6

Suicide Rates (per 100,000 per year) In 1970 And Changes By 1980 For The Total Population And For Those Aged 15-24

	total population		youth	
	1970	% change	1970	% change
Australia	12.4	-11.2%	8.6	+30.2%
Austria	24.2	+6.2%	16.5	+9.1%
Bulgaria	11.9	+14.3%	6.9	+34.8%
Canada	11.3	+23.9%	10.2	+50.0%
Chile	6.0	-18.3%	10.1	-31.7%
Denmark	21.5	+47.0%	8.5	+42.4%
Finland	21.3	+20.7%	14.7	+60.5%
France	15.4	+26.0%	7.0	+52.9%
Germany West	21.3	-1.9%	13.4	-6.7%
Greece	3.2	+3.1%	1.5	+20.0%
Hong Kong	13.6	-0.7%	7.7	+1.3%
Hungary	34.8	+29.0%	18.9	+5.8%
Italy	5.8	+25.9%	2.9	+34.5%
Japan	15.2	+15.8%	13.0	-3.8%
Netherlands	8.1	+24.7%	4.0	+50.0%
New Zealand	9.6	+12.5%	8.0	+73.7%
Norway	8.4	+47.6%	3.7	+224.3%
Portugal	7.5	-1.3%	4.5	+2.2%
Singapore	8.9	+25.8%	7.8	+32.1%
Spain	4.2	+4.8%	1.4	+92.9%
Sweden	22.3	-13.0%	13.3	-13.5%
Switzerland	18.6	+38.2%	13.0	+80.0%
Thailand	4.2	+76.2%	7.2	+77.8%
UK: England & Wales	8.0	+10.0%	6.0	+6.7%
Scotland	7.6	+31.6%	5.8	+65.5%
USA	11.5	+2.6%	8.8	+39.8%
Venezuela	6.8	-23.5%	14.5	-28.3%

Australia, Canada, France, Greece, Italy, Thailand and the United States. Nations with a rising youth suicide rate only in females were Austria, Bulgaria, England and Wales and Singapore.

Lester (1988) examined the association between some social indicators and youth suicide rates and found that the associations for youth suicide rates were sometimes different than for the overall suicide rates. For example, whereas Lester found that the overall suicide rate was greater in nations with a higher quality of life, youth suicide rates were not related to the quality of life. In addition, whereas the overall suicide rate rose more from 1970 to 1980 in nations with the higher suicide rates in 1970, this was not true for youth suicide rates.

In order to explore the correlates of a rising youth suicide rate further, the twenty nine nations with data on youth suicide in 1970 and 1980 reported in Lester (1988) were studied. Data on the nations for 1970 were obtained as follows: population, percentages of the population 0-14, 15-64 and 65+, urban population percentage, population density per square kilometer of total land and of agricultural land, the crude death and birth rates, the life expectancy, and the infant mortality rate from the World Bank (1984), the real gross domestic product per capita from Summers and Heston (1984), total suicide and homicide rates from the World Health Organization (annual), the marriage rate from the United Nations (1984), the area of the nation from Hammond (1967), and the alcohol consumption rate from Adrian (1984).

The youth suicide rate in 1970 was significantly associated only with the total suicide rate (Pearson r = 0.77, two-tailed $p < .001$). The percentage change in the youth suicide rate was significantly associated only with the life expectancy (r = 0.42, $p < .05$), the infant mortality rate (r = -0.44, $p < .05$), and the youth suicide rate (r = -0.36, $p < .05$).

Table 13.7

Factor analysis of the social variables and the correlates of the factor scores with the change in youth suicide rates

	FACTOR			
	I	II	III	IV
population	.03	-.11	.72*	.01
% young	-.93*	.24	-.02	-.17
% adults	.90*	-.08	.06	.14
% elderly	.83*	-.43	-.03	.17
% urban	.27	.69*	.33	.06
population density	-.10	.88*	-.28	.04
density/agricultual land	-.11	.87*	-.28	.05
birth rate	-.95*	-.04	-.04	-.17
death rate	-.12	-.80*	-.21	.37
life expectancy	.93*	.24	.18	-.03
gross domestic product	.60*	-.08	.60*	.29
suicide rate	.47	-.09	-.06	.84*
homicide rate	-.90*	-.25	.08	.02
infant mortality	-.82*	-.33	-.22	-.09
marriage rate	.60*	-.01	.51*	-.11
area	-.04	.04	.86*	.01
alcohol consumption	.57*	-.43	.03	.06
youth suicide rate	.01	-.01	.11	.94*
percentage of variance	41.9%	18.8%	11.4%	8.9%
Pearson r with change in youth suicide rate	0.34#	-0.06	0.02	-0.36#

two-tailed p < .05
* high loading (> 0.50)

The social variables were subjected a factor analysis using SPSSX, with a Principal Components extraction and a varimax rotation, and four factors extracted (see Table 13.7). Factor I which appears to measure age and Factor IV which appears to measure the suicide rate were both associated with the change in the youth suicide rate giving a multiple R of 0.50, accounting for 25 percent of the variance in the change in the youth suicide rate.

The results are scanty. Only two correlates were found for the change in the youth suicide rates of nations from 1970 to 1980, namely the nation's infant mortality rate and the life expectancy. Nations with a greater life expectancy and a lower infant mortality rate experienced a greater increase in their youth suicide rate.

The limited results of this analysis, though disappointing, are not surprising. Lester (1988) noted that national youth suicide rates show fewer associations with social variables than total suicide rates, suggesting that youth suicide rates have different social determinants from the suicide rates of other age groups and may require different explanatory theories.

Suicide in Children

Looking at the suicide rates of those aged 5-14, Barraclough (1987) found that the female rates were as high or higher than the male rates in fourteen nations, mainly in South America and Asia. This is surprising since the overall male suicide rates are higher than the overall female suicide rates in almost all nations of the world.

Lester (1990) calculated the sex ratio for the suicide rate for each age group for 31 nations for 1980. The sex ratios for those aged 5-14 and 15-24 were positively associated as were those for the older age groups. However, the sex ratios for the younger age groups were not associated with the sex ratios for the older groups. The dividing group was those aged 25-34 for whom the sex ratio was associated with both those of the younger and the older groups.

The association between the sex ratio for suicide and the gross domestic product per capita was positive for the younger age groups and negative for the older age groups. Lester concluded that the sex ratio for suicide rates may be differently determined in younger and older adults.

Table 13.8

Elderly Suicide Rates In 1970 And The Change By 1980

	males				females			
	total		elderly		total		elderly	
	rate	change	rate	change	rate	change	rate	change
Australia	17.0	-3.5%	38.5	-17.1%	7.6	-26.3%	9.5	-4.2%
Austria	35.5	+6.5%	77.7	+10.3%	14.2	+4.9%	29.4	+15.3%
Bulgaria	16.1	+18.6%	108.3	+0.4%	7.7	+6.5%	34.5	-7.5%
Canada	16.2	+31.5%	24.6	+54.9%	6.4	+6.2%	4.6	+28.3%
Chile	9.6	-12.5%	19.9	+6.5%	1.9	-26.3%	3.5	-31.4%
Denmark	27.4	+50.0%	55.0	+47.8%	15.7	+42.0%	19.1	+65.4%
England/Wales	9.5	+15.8%	23.9	-9.6%	6.6	+1.5%	9.7	+13.4%
Finland	34.4	+20.9%	50.5	+19.0%	9.2	+16.3%	7.4	+31.1%
France	22.8	+22.8%	74.4	+33.9%	8.4	+32.1%	18.6	+31.2%
Greece	4.6	+2.2%	11.6	+43.1%	1.8	+5.6%	5.6	+8.9%
Guatemala	5.3	-60.4%	5.0	-44.0%	1.0	-70.0%	4.3	-100.0%
Hong Kong	15.5	-5.2%	88.7	-29.0%	11.8	+2.5%	89.1	-27.5%
Hungary	50.8	+27.0%	146.4	+38.1%	19.8	+33.8%	76.4	+18.6%
Israel	6.9	+17.4%	17.0	+115.3%	4.6	-17.4%	7.5	+206.7%
Italy	8.1	+24.7%	33.3	+12.3%	3.5	+31.4%	7.8	+30.8%
Japan	17.2	+29.1%	82.1	-10.7%	13.2	-0.8%	66.3	-9.2%
Hetherlands	9.9	+29.3%	42.5	-3.3%	6.2	+19.4%	17.5	-31.4%
New Zealand	12.6	+14.3%	31.2	+14.1%	6.6	+7.6%	11.1	+60.4%
Norway	11.8	+55.1%	13.3	+80.5%	5.0	+32.0%	1.9	+147.4%
Portugal	11.9	-5.9%	72.2	-25.6%	3.4	+14.7%	11.7	-6.0%
Scotland	9.5	+35.8%	21.7	+6.9%	6.0	+21.7%	5.6	+44.6%
Singapore	10.6	+17.0%	137.9	-22.1%	7.1	+40.8%	53.6	+6.9%
Spain	6.3	+6.3%	29.0	-1.7%	2.2	+0.0%	6.9	-7.2%
Sweden	31.3	-11.8%	48.8	+0.2%	13.2	-14.4%	13.0	-12.3%
Switzerland	27.4	+33.9%	74.1	+8.9%	10.1	+50.5%	16.0	+45.0%
USA	16.7	+11.4%	41.8	+4.1%	6.5	-16.9%	6.7	-19.4%
Venezuela	9.5	-11.6%	47.5	-1.5%	4.0	-50.0%	5.3	-47.2%
West Germany	28.2	+0.4%	75.2	-3.2%	15.0	-6.0%	27.0	-4.1%

Elderly Suicide Rates

As noted above, there has been concern over possible rising elderly suicide rates in recent years. The changes in the elderly suicide rates for those aged 75 and older are shown in Table 13.8. It can be seen for elderly men, the suicide rate rose rose during the 1970s in in 17 nations and declined in 11. The direction of the change was in the same direction for the total suicide rate and the elderly suicide rate in 20 nations and in opposite directions in eight.

For elderly women, the suicide rate rose in 15 nations and declined in 13. The direction of the change was in the same direction for the total suicide rate and the elderly suicide rate in 22 nations and in opposite directions in six. Comparing the elderly men and women, the direction of change was the same in 22 nations and in opposite directions in six.

In several nations, the size of the change was similar for the elderly and the total population. For example, in Finland, the total male suicide rate rose 20.9% and the elderly male suicide rate rose 19.0%. In some nations, the change in the elderly suicide rate was much greater. For example, in Israel, the total male suicide rate rose 17.4% while the elderly male suicide rate rose 115.3%. In some nations, the reverse was true. For example, In Hong Kong, the total female suicide rate rose 2.5% while the elderly female suicide rate dropped 27.5%.

Thus, there was considerable variation in the changes in elderly suicide rates by nation. The percentage changes in the elderly suicide rates for men and for women were, however, associated ($r = 0.57$, one-tailed $p < .001$).

Although the percentage change in the total male suicide rate was associated with the gross national product per capita, the quality of life, the percentage of elderely, the divorce rate and the total suicide rate, none of these variables were associated with the percentage change in the elderly men's suicide rate (see Table 13.9). The same was true for women's suicide rates. Thus, no predictors of changes in the elderly suicide rate were identified.

Table 13.9

Correlates Of Changes In The Elderly Suicide Rate

	males		females	
	total	elderly	total	elderly
gnp/capita	0.45*	0.21	0.22	0.21
quality of life	0.52*	0.11	0.51*	0.15
divorce rate	0.33*	0.22	0.13	0.13
total suicide rate	0.31	0.08	0.38*	0.06
percentage of elderly	0.46*	0.25	0.52*	0.29
multiple R	0.58	0.31	0.59	0.32

* one-tailed p < .05 or better

It appears, therefore, that changes in the elderly suicide rate vary considerably from nation to nation and that correlates of these changes cannot yet be identified.

Table 13.10

Homicide Rates In 1975 And The Age Group With The Highest Risk Of Being Murdered

Non-European	homicide rate	age group with highest risk	Europe	homicide rate	age group with highest risk
Australia	1.6	25-34	Austria	1.6	0-1
Canada	2.7	25-34	Belgium	0.9	75+
Chile	2.1	0-1	Bulgaria	2.3	75+
Costa Rica	4.8	75+	Czechoslovakia	1.3	0-1
Cuba	4.0	15-24/25-34	Denmark	0.6	0-1
Dominican Republic	4.7	25-34	England & Wales	1.0	0-1
Egypt	1.2	75+	Finland	3.6	35-44
Hong Kong	0.9	25-34/55-64	France	1.0	35-44
Israel	1.3	75+	Germany, West	1.2	0-1
Japan	1.3	0-1	Greece	0.8	25-34
New Zealand	1.1	45-54	Hungary	2.0	0-1
Nicaragua	18.6	25-34	Ireland	1.0	0-1
Paraguay	14.8	25-34	Italy	1.3	35-44
Philippines	1.4	35-44	Netherlands	0.7	0-1
Puerto Rico	16.1	25-34	Northern Ireland	11.4	25-34
Singapore	1.9	65+	Norway	0.7	0-1
Thailand	30.2	35-44	Poland	1.0	0-1
Trinidad & Tobago	5.1	45-54	Portugal	1.9	15-24
USA	10.0	25-34	Scotland	1.5	0-1
Uruguay	2.9	0-1	Spain	0.6	45-54
Venezuela	7.8	25-34	Sweden	1.1	25-34
			Switzerland	0.9	0-1

Table 13.11

Homicide Rates By Age In Countries Of The World In 1970, 1980 And 1988

	Age									
	0-1	1-4	5-14	15-24	25-34	35-44	45-54	55-64	65-74	75+
Australia										
1970 male	3.8	0.8	0.6	1.8	2.9	2.4	2.2	1.3	0.3	0.7
1980 male	5.2	1.7	0.5	2.1	3.9	3.2	1.5	2.5	2.4	1.7
1988 male	1.6	1.2	0.6	3.6	4.4	4.1	3.2	2.6	2.0	3.1
1970 female	3.2	0.9	1.1	0.8	1.6	2.6	1.1	1.3	1.9	0.4
1980 female	2.7	0.9	0.2	2.7	2.2	1.9	1.8	1.3	1.0	0.0
1988 female	5.0	1.7	0.7	2.9	2.7	2.3	2.0	0.5	0.5	1.2
Austria										
1970 male	13.8	0.0	1.0	2.8	1.4	1.4	0.9	2.4	2.1	2.6
1980 male	4.3	2.3	0.5	1.1	1.9	1.2	2.2	1.7	1.5	0.7
1988 male	11.0	1.1	0.0	0.6	2.4	2.6	1.3	0.8	0.9	1.2
1970 female	7.3	1.2	0.5	0.8	1.6	0.7	1.3	1.4	1.4	2.6
1980 female	0.0	1.2	0.6	1.5	1.0	1.0	0.5	0.7	0.9	2.3
1988 female	0.0	0.0	0.2	1.0	1.2	2.6	1.1	0.4	0.3	1.9
Bulgaria										
1970 male	1.4	0.0	0.3	3.6	4.7	3.4	4.6	5.5	5.6	3.9
1980 male	1.5	0.4	0.5	4.0	6.2	4.1	5.8	3.8	3.9	3.4
1988 male	0.0	0.8	0.3	3.7	5.6	4.1	4.8	4.4	2.9	7.5
1970 female	3.0	0.4	0.2	1.2	1.0	1.4	1.6	1.3	0.0	2.8
1980 female	4.8	0.0	0.3	1.8	1.5	0.7	1.3	1.5	0.8	4.1
1988 female	3.5	1.7	0.3	0.7	2.3	1.6	1.6	1.0	3.2	3.3
Canada										
1970 male	2.1	1.3	0.7	2.7	4.1	3.3	3.2	3.7	3.5	1.8
1980 male	3.2	0.8	0.4	2.2	4.5	4.9	3.2	2.4	2.9	3.3
1988 male	3.1	0.5	0.5	2.6	3.9	3.3	3.5	1.9	2.2	2.1
1970 female	4.4	0.7	0.7	1.6	2.4	2.0	1.6	1.3	1.5	1.9
1980 female	0.6	1.0	0.4	1.6	2.0	1.3	1.6	1.4	1.5	0.6
1988 female	2.2	1.0	0.3	1.6	2.3	1.3	1.5	0.7	0.4	1.0
Denmark										
1970 male	0.0	1.2	0.3	0.5	0.9	0.0	1.0	1.1	0.6	1.1
1980 male	0.0	2.3	1.3	1.3	1.7	0.6	1.1	0.4	1.0	0.9
1988 male	0.0	0.9	0.6	2.2	1.5	1.0	1.3	0.0	0.0	0.8
1970 female	0.0	1.3	0.3	1.0	1.5	0.4	0.3	0.4	0.0	1.6

1980 female	7.2	1.6	0.3	1.9	1.0	1.5	3.3	0.7	1.2	1.7
1988 female	3.5	2.8	0.7	0.5	1.9	1.5	1.0	0.8	0.0	1.8
<u>Finland</u>										
1970 male	15.1	0.0	0.3	3.6	3.9	5.3	5.6	2.4	2.6	2.5
1980 male	3.1	1.5	0.0	4.3	6.4	7.8	8.9	6.4	2.7	5.0
1988 male	6.2	0.0	0.0	2.3	5.8	7.1	5.7	4.6	2.1	2.4
1970 female	6.3	3.0	0.3	0.7	0.6	1.0	2.1	0.4	0.6	2.5
1980 female	9.8	2.4	0.0	0.8	3.2	3.0	1.1	1.9	0.9	0.7
1988 female	0.0	0.0	0.0	0.9	2.4	1.5	5.4	1.5	0.9	2.1
<u>France</u>										
1970 male	1.8	0.2	0.2	0.5	1.6	1.4	1.5	1.4	0.9	0.9
1980 male	0.7	0.5	0.4	1.4	1.5	1.9	1.5	1.2	1.1	1.4
1988 male	2.3	0.7	0.3	1.2	1.6	1.6	1.7	1.1	1.0	1.4
1970 female	1.2	0.2	0.1	0.5	0.7	0.7	0.7	0.4	0.4	1.3
1980 female	1.3	0.4	0.3	0.7	0.9	1.1	0.5	0.6	0.9	2.0
1988 female	2.9	0.8	0.2	0.5	0.8	1.2	0.9	0.7	0.8	1.1
<u>Greece</u>										
1970 male	1.3	0.3	0.1	0.8	0.9	1.2	0.7	1.7	1.4	1.5
1980 male	0.0	0.0	0.1	0.7	2.1	1.5	1.4	0.9	0.5	0.0
1988 male	0.0	0.4	0.3	0.9	3.3	1.8	2.5	0.9	1.2	2.8
1970 female	0.0	0.0	0.0	0.8	0.2	0.1	0.4	0.2	0.6	0.5
1980 female	1.4	0.4	0.3	0.6	0.9	0.3	0.0	0.2	0.2	1.1
1988 female	3.9	0.4	0.0	1.0	0.7	1.4	0.2	0.3	0.7	0.3
<u>Hungary</u>										
1970 male	6.4	1.4	0.5	1.9	4.4	3.1	3.9	2.5	1.9	5.2
1980 male	11.8	1.1	0.4	1.9	3.7	5.1	4.9	4.1	4.7	5.7
1988 male	17.2	1.6	1.0	2.3	4.1	4.1	5.9	2.9	3.4	5.0
1970 female	10.9	1.8	0.3	1.3	1.1	0.9	1.3	1.5	1.1	2.2
1980 female	17.9	1.2	0.4	1.4	1.9	2.6	1.4	1.9	1.3	2.6
1988 female	8.3	3.3	0.8	1.3	2.9	2.3	1.2	1.6	1.7	2.9
<u>Italy</u>										
1970 male	0.6	0.2	0.4	1.0	1.7	1.8	1.5	1.0	1.3	1.2
1980 male	0.6	0.3	0.4	3.2	5.2	4.5	4.2	3.3	1.7	2.1
1988 male	0.7	0.1	0.2	3.2	6.1	4.9	3.7	3.0	2.2	1.8
1970 female	1.4	0.2	0.2	0.5	0.8	0.8	0.8	0.4	0.5	0.2
1980 female	1.3	0.2	0.3	0.8	1.2	0.7	1.0	0.9	0.8	1.1
1988 female	0.0	0.3	0.2	0.6	0.8	0.7	0.7	0.6	0.5	0.7
<u>Japan</u>										

1970 male	8.0	2.6	0.9	1.4	2.3	2.0	1.7	1.0	0.9	0.6
1980 male	6.2	2.0	0.9	0.3	1.1	1.5	1.3	0.7	0.9	1.3
1988 male	5.2	1.1	0.5	0.6	0.5	1.0	1.3	0.8	0.5	0.8
1970 female	8.8	2.0	0.9	0.4	0.8	0.8	0.5	0.7	0.8	1.3
1980 female	5.9	2.0	0.7	0.4	0.7	0.7	0.7	0.4	0.6	0.7
1988 female	5.5	1.5	0.4	0.4	0.4	0.7	0.6	0.5	0.7	1.1

Netherlands

1970 male	1.6	0.2	0.1	0.9	1.1	1.0	0.6	0.9	0.3	0.5
1980 male	2.2	0.3	0.1	1.4	1.4	1.6	0.9	0.6	1.2	0.8
1988 male	1.0	0.8	0.2	1.2	2.1	1.4	1.3	0.6	0.4	0.7
1970 female	1.7	0.0	0.2	0.5	0.4	0.4	0.1	0.0	0.4	0.7
1980 female	0.0	0.6	0.4	0.5	1.0	0.8	0.1	0.3	0.7	0.5
1988 female	4.4	1.4	0.2	0.5	1.0	0.7	0.8	0.8	0.0	0.8

Norway

1970 male	0.0	1.5	0.3	0.3	1.7	0.5	1.6	0.5	1.4	1.3
1980 male	0.0	0.9	0.0	1.6	2.2	2.1	1.0	1.3	0.0	3.3
1988 male	0.0	0.0	0.4	2.3	2.2	4.1	2.4	1.0	1.7	0.0
1970 female	0.0	0.8	0.3	0.3	0.4	1.0	0.0	0.0	0.6	0.0
1980 female	0.0	0.0	0.6	0.7	1.7	0.9	2.4	1.2	0.5	0.0
1988 female	0.0	0.0	0.0	0.6	0.3	1.0	0.5	0.5	0.5	0.5

Portugal

1970 male	1.[illegible]	0.3	0.1	0.3	1.0	2.0	1.5	1.2	1.7	1.9
1980 male	2.4	0.3	0.0	1.6	2.8	3.9	3.6	2.2	2.0	4.0
1988 male	0.0	0.0	0.1	1.7	3.9	2.1	3.2	1.8	3.2	2.6
1970 female	1.2	0.3	0.1	0.6	0.3	0.5	0.5	0.6	1.5	1.1
1980 female	1.3	0.3	0.1	0.7	0.8	0.8	0.8	0.8	0.8	0.5
1988 female	6.8	0.4	0.1	0.4	0.4	1.2	0.8	1.2	0.9	0.6

Switzerland

1970 male	11.7	1.0	0.0	0.6	0.9	0.8	1.8	0.0	0.5	1.1
1980 male	2.7	1.4	0.7	0.4	0.8	0.5	1.4	0.3	1.3	0.0
1988 male	7.3	3.3	0.5	1.2	1.7	2.0	1.5	1.2	0.0	1.3
1970 female	6.3	0.5	0.2	0.6	0.5	0.3	0.6	0.6	0.7	0.6
1980 female	2.8	1.5	0.7	2.0	1.4	1.4	0.3	1.5	0.3	0.5
1988 female	2.6	0.7	0.0	1.0	1.6	1.8	0.7	0.6	0.7	0.7

UK: England & Wales

1970 male	6.2	1.1	0.1	1.1	1.3	0.9	0.3	0.6	0.6	1.0
1980 male	0.9	0.8	0.2	1.1	1.4	1.1	1.0	0.9	0.6	0.9
1988 male	4.5	0.8	0.1	0.7	1.0	0.8	0.8	0.8	0.3	0.5

1970 female	4.5	0.9	0.3	0.6	0.7	0.5	0.4	0.5	0.5	1.0
1980 female	3.1	0.7	0.3	0.9	1.0	0.8	0.6	0.6	0.7	1.0
1988 female	1.5	0.6	0.3	0.7	0.4	0.6	0.4	0.6	0.1	0.5

UK: Scotland

1970 male	2.2	1.1	0.0	2.3	3.0	2.1	0.7	0.7	0.0	1.4
1980 male	0.0	0.8	0.2	3.9	2.8	2.4	2.1	2.8	1.0	3.7
1988 male	0.0	1.5	0.0	6.1	9.8	6.8	7.9	5.1	1.6	0.0
1970 female	7.1	1.1	0.0	0.5	1.3	0.7	0.6	0.0	0.4	0.7
1980 female	9.0	0.0	0.5	0.9	0.3	1.3	1.3	1.0	1.1	1.1
1988 female	6.2	1.6	0.6	1.2	2.4	1.5	1.4	1.0	1.2	0.9

USA

1970 male	4.2	1.8	1.0	189.	27.3	22.2	16.9	12.3	8.7	6.1
1980 male	6.2	2.7	1.2	24.0	31.6	24.3	18.4	11.8	9.2	7.9
1988 male	7.5	2.9	1.5	24.4	24.2	17.0	11.2	8.1	5.9	6.5
1970 female	3.9	1.9	0.7	4.6	6.0	5.7	3.6	2.5	2.2	2.6
1980 female	5.5	2.2	1.1	6.6	6.9	5.7	4.1	2.8	3.0	3.7
1988 female	8.6	2.3	1.1	6.0	7.3	4.6	3.1	2.5	2.9	3.5

West Germany

1970 male	5.8	1.2	0.6	1.5	2.5	1.9	2.0	1.6	1.5	1.3
1980 male	4.7	0.8	0.5	1.0	1.9	1.9	1.7	1.0	1.0	1.3
1988 male	3.7	0.8	0.5	0.7	1.2	1.7	1.2	0.9	1.0	1.6
1970 female	6.1	1.1	0.8	1.6	1.3	1.1	1.3	0.6	0.6	1.2
1980 female	5.3	0.9	0.4	1.0	1.5	1.1	0.7	0.9	0.5	1.6
1988 female	2.1	0.8	0.7	1.1	1.3	1.7	1.0	0.5	0.4	1.3

HOMICIDE RATES

Lester (1986a) examined the age distribution of homicide victims in nations of the world in 1975 (see Table 13.10). Outside of Europe, the risk of being murdered was usually greatest for young adults (in twelve of the twenty-one nations). In contrast, in Europe, twelve of the twenty-two nations had infants at the greatest risk for being murdered. In seven other European nations, young adults were at greatest risk. The full homicide rates by age for 1970, 1980 and 1988 for nations with data available are shown in Table 13.11.

Nations with infants at high risk tended to have lower homicide rates than those with young adults at high risk. Nations with high homicide rates appear to have a large proportion of young adults killed. As the homicide rate is reduced, young adults become relatively less at risk. In a study of industrialized nations, Lester (1974) found that the murder rate of infants was associated with the *suicide* rate of the nations, not the homicide rates. (Infanticide is typically carried out by a parent who often commits suicide afterwards [Lester, 1986b].) The murder of infants is explored in greater depth in Chapter 16.

In six countries (Belgium, Bulgaria, Costa Rica, Egypt, Israel, and Singapore) the eldest were at greatest risk of being murdered.

DISCUSSION

Often researchers report epidemiological trends in suicide and homicide rates for their own nation. Broadening our perspective by looking at these trends in many nations give us an idea about general epidemiological trends which can be found in the majority of nations of the world. Scholars should first explain these general trends before attempting to account for exceptions to such trends.

REFERENCES

Barraclough, B. M. Sex ratio of juvenile suicide. *Journal of the American Academy of Child & Adolescent Psychiatry*, 1987, 26, 434-435.

Fusé, T. To be or not to be. *Stress* 1980, 1(3), 18-25.

Girard, C. Age, gender, and suicide. *American Sociological Review*, 1993, 58, 553-574.

Lester, D. A cross-national study of suicide and homicide. *Behavior Science Research*, 1974, 9, 307-318.

Lester, D. The distribution of sex and age among completed suicides. *International Journal of Social Psychiatry*, 1982, 28, 256-260.

Lester, D. The distribution of sex and age among victims of homicide. *International Journal of Social Psychiatry*, 1986a, 32(2), 47-50.

Lester, D. *The murderer and his murder*. New York: AMS, 1986b.

Lester, D. Youth suicide: a cross-cultural perspective. *Adolescence*, 1988, 23, 955-958.

Lester, D. The sex distribution of suicides by age in nations of the world. *Social Psychiatry & Psychiatric Epidemiology*, 1990, 25, 87-88.

Lester, D. Age distribution among suicides in nations of the world. *Perceptual & Motor Skills*, 1993, 77, 1386.

Chapter 14

Suicide, Homicide and the Quality of Life

Common sense suggests that, as we improve conditions in the world, people should be much happier. If we can eliminate poverty and oppressive forces (such as sexism and racism), if we clean up the environment, if we improve the educational and cultural offerings for our citizens, if we do all this, then we should be much happier.

Unfortunately, there is a sociological theory that predicts exactly the opposite of this. Henry and Short (1954) argued that when we have clear external sources to blame for our failures and our unhappiness then we will feel angry and be outwardly aggressive. In constrast, if there is no clear external source to blame for our failures and unhappiness, then we will hold ourselves responsible. In this case, we are more likely to feel depressed and guilty, increasing the risk that we may kill ourselves. In both the USA and South Africa, for example, the oppressed (blacks) have the higher homicide rates, while the oppressors (whites) have the higher suicide rates (Lester, 1971).

There is a great deal of evidence to support this idea. In a study in the USA, Lester (1986) found that the states in the USA with the highest quality of life (rated on a variety of aspects) had the highest suicide rates and the lowest homicide rates. Similarly, in a study of nations of the world, Lester (1984) found that nations with the highest quality of life had the highest suicide rates and the lowest homicide rates. It appears that if life is better, suicide becomes more common and homicide less common.

Table 14.1

Measurement Of The Quality Of Life

Education:
- school enrollment
- pupil-teacher ratio
- percent adult illiteracy
- percent gnp in education

Health:
- infant mortality rate
- population per physician
- male life expectancy at age 1

Women's Status:
- percent girls attending first level schools
- percent children in primary school who are female
- percent adult female illiteracy
- years since women's suffrage
- years since women suffrage equal to men

Defense Effort:
- percent gnp for defense spending

Economy:
- economic growth rate
- per capita income
- average annual rate of inflation
- per capita food production

Demography:
- total population
- crude birth rate
- crude death rate
- rate of population increase
- percent of population under 15 years

Geography:
- percent arable land mass
- number major natural disaster impacts
- lives lost in major natural disasters

Political Stability:
- number of political protest demonstrations
- number of political riots
- number of political strikes
- number of armed attacks
- rate of death from domestic violence

Political Participation:
- years since independence
- years since most recent constitution
- presence of functioning parliamentary system
- presence of functioning political party system
- degree of influence of military
- number of popular elections held

Cultural Diversity:
- largest percent sharing same mother tongue
- largest percent sharing same basic religious belief
- ethnic-linguistic fractionalization index

Welfare Effort:
- years since first law for:
  - old age, invalidity, death
  - sickness and maternity
  - work injury
  - unemployment
  - family allowances

Lester in his study of nations of the world used ratings by Estes (1984) of the quality of life. Estes, however, used several components for his overall rating of the quality of life, including education, health status and women's status. (See Table 14.1 for a complete list of the components.) The present study extended Lester's earlier report by exploring the association between each component of the overall quality of life and rates of personal violence, exploring the relationship between changes in the overall quality of life and changes in rates of personal violence over time, and exploring these associations for a sample of all nations of the world with available data and separately for a sample of the most industrialized nations.[12]

Ratings of the overall quality of life for nations of the world in 1969 and 1979 and for the components of the quality of life in 1979 were obtained from Estes (1984). Rates of suicide and homicide for 1970 and 1980 were obtained from the World Health Organization (1973-1984).

Table 14.2

The Association Between The Quality Of Life And Rates Of Personal Violence

	18 nations		43 nations	
	suicide rate	homicide rate	suicide rate	homicide rate
quality of life	0.30	-0.68***	0.57***	-0.50***
education	-0.16	0.12	0.38**	-0.58***
health	0.25	-0.28	0.46***	-0.63***
women's status	-0.23	0.11	0.34*	-0.31*
defense effort	0.24	-0.41*	0.16	0.17
economy	0.34	0.36	0.22	-0.07
demography	0.57**	-0.68***	0.61***	-0.56***
geography	0.06	-0.87***	0.21	-0.46***
political stability	0.43*	-0.15	0.16	0.11
political participation	-0.29	0.14	0.18	-0.17
cultural diversity	0.07	-0.22	-0.04	-0.21
welfare effort	0.08	-0.54*	0.49***	-0.48***

* one-tailed p < 0.05
** one-tailed p < 0.01
*** one-tailed p < 0.001

[12] The nations used were those used by Lynn (1971): Australia, Austria, Belgium, Canada, Denmark, Finland, France, Ireland, Italy, Japan, the Netherlands, New Zealand, Norway, Sweden, Switzerland, the United Kingdom, the USA, and West Germany.

The data were first analyzed for a sample of 43 nations whose populations in 1980 were greater than one million and for which data were available. The Pearson correlations between the components of the quality of life and rates of personal violence for 1980 are shown in Table 14.2.

For the complete sample of 43 nations, only five of the eleven components of the quality of life index correlated with suicide rates and only six of the components correlated with homicide rates. Interestingly, defense efforts, the economy, political stability, political participation and cultural diversity were not correlated with rates of personal violence. The strongest correlates were the education, health and demographic components.

For the reduced sample of industrialized nations, even fewer components correlated with the rates of personal violence, though the associations were more consistent for homicide rates than for suicide rates.

Table 14.3

The Association Between Components Of The Quality Of Life And Rates Of Personal Violence For 43 Nations In 1980

	FACTOR			
	I	II	III	IV
education	0.80*	-0.10	0.02	-0.07
health	0.91*	-0.11	0.01	-0.09
women's status	0.68*	-0.23	0.20	0.34
defense effort	-0.04	0.06	0.80*	0.26
economy	0.27	0.07	0.61*	-0.50*
demography	0.90*	0.06	0.01	-0.04
geography	0.46*	0.43*	-0.33	0.12
political stability	-0.10	0.79*	0.24	-0.06
political participation	0.50*	-0.65*	0.21	-0.25
cultural diversity	0.12	0.09	0.12	0.80*
welfare effort	0.86*	-0.11	0.01	0.25
percent of variance	38%	13%	11%	10%
correlation with				
suicide rate	0.55#	0.20	0.17	-0.07
homicide rate	-0.65#	-0.11	0.22	-0.07

* a high loading on the factor (greater than 0.40)
\# one-tailed significance less than 0.001

For the total sample of 43 nations, a factor analysis of the components of the quality of life (using a Principal Components extraction and a varimax rotation in SPSSX) identified four factors, only one of which correlated with rates of personal violence (see Table 14.3). This factor (Factor I) had the strongest loadings from health, demography, welfare and education. A similar factor analysis for the 18 industrialized nations identified five factors, only one of which correlated with homicide rates (see Table 14.4). This factor had high loadings from geography, welfare effort and demography.

Table 14.4

The Association Between Components Of The Quality Of Life And Rates Of Personal Violence For 18 Nations In 1980

	FACTOR				
	I	II	III	IV	V
education	-0.10	-0.01	0.60*	0.28	0.37
health	0.06	0.06	-0.14	0.90*	-0.14
women's status	0.01	0.02	-0.06	-0.04	0.94*
defense effort	0.10	0.89*	-0.11	-0.12	-0.15
economy	-0.38	0.09	0.29	0.65*	0.28
demography	0.69*	0.45*	-0.04	0.39	-0.16
geography	0.94*	0.13	-0.02	-0.15	-0.14
political stability	-0.02	0.85*	-0.01	0.38	0.18
political participation	-0.07	-0.60*	0.68*	0.01	-0.20
cultural diversity	0.12	0.05	-0.92*	0.18	0.14
welfare effort	0.87*	-0.17	-0.22	-0.09	0.26
percent of variance	28%	21%	13%	12%	10%
correlation with					
suicide rate	0.14	0.37	-0.06	0.38	-0.18
homicide rate	-0.81#	-0.24	0.08	-0.11	0.20

* high loading (greater than 0.40)
\# one-tailed significance less than 0.001

Examination of changes in these variables revealed that changes in the quality of life from 1969 to 1979 were not associated with suicide rates in 1980 or changes in suicide rates during the 1970s (see Table 14.5). However, for the industrialized nations, increases in the quality of life were associated with greater increases in the homicide rates during the 1970s and higher homicide rates in 1980.

Table 14.5

Correlations Between Changes In The Quality Of Life And Changes In Rates Of Personal Violence From 1970 To 1980

	change in suicide rate	change in homicide rate	1980 suicide rate	1980 homicide rate
39 nations	0.03	0.07	0.07	0.06
18 nations	0.14	0.44*	0.07	0.60**

* one-tailed $p < 0.05$
** one-tailed $p < 0.01$

Discussion

The present results indicated that the general associations identified by Lester between the quality of life and rates of personal violence holds only for some components of the quality of life index, in particular, education, health, demography and welfare effort. These components are concerned with the psychological welfare of the individual (as compared to components such as geography, cultural diversity and the defense effort).

Interestingly, the results differed for the smaller sample of industrialized nations. In these nations, the quality of life (and its components) were much less strongly associated with suicide rates, while still showing some relationship to homicide rates. Since the quality of life is much higher in the industrialized nations, it appears that, at high levels of quality, other variables determine suicide rates.

Changes in the quality of life from 1969 to 1979 were quite small. The correlation between the two sets of ratings in 1969 and 1979 was 0.92 for the 43 nations and 0.90 for the industrialized nations. The mean quality of life for the 43 nations in 1979 was 145.2 and the mean increase from 1969 to 1979 was only 2.2. (For the industrialized nations, the mean quality of life in 1979 was 173.6 and the mean increase from 1969 to 1979 2.6.) It would be interesting to explore the relationship between changes in the quality of life and rates of personal violence over a time period in which greater changes took place in the quality of life.

References

Estes, R. J. *The social progress of nations.* New York: Praeger, 1984.

Henry, A. F., & Short, J. F. *Suicide and homicide.* New York: Free Press, 1954.

Lester, D. Suicide and homicide in open and closed societies. *Psychological Reports*, 1971, 29, 430.

Lester, D. The association between the quality of life and suicide and homicide rates. *Journal of Social Psychology*, 1984, 124, 247-248.

Lester, D. Suicide, homicide, and the quality of life. *Suicide & Life-Threatening Behavior*, 1986, 16, 389-392.

Lynn, R. *Personality and national character.* Oxford: Pergamon, 1971.

World Health Organization. *Statistics annual.* Geneva, Switzerland: World Health Organization, 1973-1984.

CHAPTER 15

MURDERING BABIES

The murder of babies during the first year of their life appears to be a phenomenon very different from murder in general. For example, in a study of 18 industrialized nations, Lester (1974) found that the murder rate of babies was associated with the *suicide* rate of the nations rather than the *murder* rate. Similarly, Christoffel, et al. (1981) found that the murder rate for babies was unrelated to the adult homicide rates of nations.

The association of national murder rates of babies with national suicide rates makes sense in view of the psychiatric research on the murder of babies which finds that the majority of babies are murdered by mothers who frequently commit suicide afterwards (Resnick, 1969). These cases appear to involve suicidal mothers who kill their babies first in order to spare the babies suffering.

A recent study by Lester (1986) showed that, outside of Europe, young adults were most likely to have the highest likelihood of being murdered of all age groups (see also Chapter 13). This was true for twelve of the twenty-one countries. In only three countries did babies have the highest likelihood of being murdered. In contrast, in Europe, twelve of the twenty-two countries had infants at the greatest risk for murder.

The countries with babies at greatest risk for murder had homicide rates lower than 2.9 per 100,000 per year. All twelve countries with a homicide rate greater than 2.9 had adults with the greatest likelihood of being murdered. Thus, babies were at high risk for murder in countries with a lower overall homicide rate.

Table 15.1

Homicide Rates For The Total Population And Babies In Nations Of The World

	homicide rates		sex ratio for homicide rates (male/female)	
	total	babies	total	babies
<u>Europe</u>				
Austria	1.5	10.7	1.38	0.96
Belgium	2.1	2.1	1.20	2.00
Bulgaria	2.2	2.2	3.09	1.42
Czechoslovakia	1.5	7.0	1.73	0.96
Denmark	0.7	0.0	1.00	0.47
Finland	2.0	10.8	3.56	0.94
France	0.7	1.5	2.00	1.14
Germany, West	1.4	5.9	1.55	1.11
Greece	0.6	0.7	3.00	3.67
Hungary	2.0	8.6	2.08	0.75
Ireland	0.4	4.7	1.33	0.55
Italy	0.8	1.0	2.20	0.87
Netherlands	0.5	1.7	2.33	1.69
Norway	0.6	0.0	2.24	-
Poland	1.1	3.5	2.00	0.98
Portugal	0.7	1.2	1.80	0.67
Spain	0.6	0.8	3.00	1.71
Sweden	0.8	1.8	1.83	0.57
Switzerland	0.7	9.1	1.50	0.65
UK: England & Wales	0.7	5.4	1.33	1.10
N. Ireland	1.2	0.0	5.25	0.00
Scotland	0.9	4.6	2.17	0.78
<u>America</u>				
Canada	2.0	3.2	1.67	1.02
Chile	3.4	6.9	10.67	0.95
Costa Rica	3.7	3.5	8.12	2.20
Cuba (1971)	4.5	4.6	2.71	0.98
El Salvador	31.2	1.7	15.58	0.89
Mexico	17.5	1.7	12.00	1.61
Panama	3.4	0.0	4.23	1.39
Puerto Rico	12.4	1.4	5.15	0.93
USA	8.2	4.0	3.91	0.97
Uruguay	3.7	4.5	8.12	1.58
Venezuela	7.9	2.0	7.21	1.65
<u>Asia</u>				
Hong Kong	1.4	0.0	3.67	3.39
Japan	1.3	8.4	1.70	0.94
Philippines	17.4	2.6	17.42	3.67
Thailand	17.6	0.3	8.72	1.42
<u>Other</u>				
Australia	1.5	3.5	1.21	0.96
Israel	1.4	3.3	1.00	1.74
New Zealand	1.2	9.6	1.08	0.94

An interesting feature of the murder of babies is that the large excess of male victims found in the overall homicide rates is much less among the babies murdered. The purpose of the present chapter was to explore the murder of babies in the nations of the world and to examine the sex ratio of the babies murdered.

The data used were for 1970, except for Cuba, Puerto Rico and Uruguay who reported data only for 1971. In order to get more reliable estimates of the sex ratio for the homicide rates of babies, a five year period was chosen (1970 to 1975 or 1971 to 1976). The countries for which data were obtained are shown in Table 15.1.[13]

Babies Versus Adults

The overall homicide rate for the nations did not differ significantly from the homicide rate for babies (mean rates 3.4 and 4.0 respectively, standard deviations 4.9 and 3.2, t = 0.61, df = 32). However, the male/female sex ratio was 3.80 for all murder victims but only 1.31 for babies (SDs 3.91 and 0.76 respectively, t = 3.96, df = 31, two-tailed p < .001). Thus, over nations, female babies are murdered at a higher rate than would be expected from the proportion of female murder victims in the nations (but still at a lower rate than male babies).

The Murder Rate for Babies

The murder rate for babies was not significantly related to the overall murder rate (Pearson r = -0.21, df = 31), but it was related to the suicide rate of the nations (r = 0.51, df = 31, p = .001). [In contrast, the overall murder rate was negatively related to the suicide rate (r = -0.39, df = 31, p = .012).]

---

13 This study is based on Lester (1991).

The Sex Ratio for Babies Murdered

The sex ratio for babies murdered was positively related to the overall homicide rate (Pearson $r = 0.38$, one-tailed $p = .01$), negatively to the murder rate of babies ($r = -0.35$, $p = .03$), and negatively to the suicide rate of the nations ($r = -0.50$, $p = .002$). Thus, male babies were murdered relatively more often and female babies relatively less often where overall homicide rates were higher, suicide rates lower, and the homicide rates for babies lower. [The sex ratio for the overall homicide rates was positively related to the overall homicide rate ($r = 0.83$, $p < .001$) but not to the homicide rate of babies ($r = -0.16$).]

The sex ratios for the overall murder rate and for the murder rate of babies were positively related ($r = 0.54$, $p = .001$).

Female Inequality

Stewart and Winter (1977) calculated indices to measure the suppression of women in various nations of the world in 1970. They developed a social-educational equality index and an economic equality index. These indices were correlated with the present data on murder.

The index of social-educational equality was significantly related to the sex ratio for the homicide rates for babies ($r = -0.33$, $p = .03$). Thus, in the nations with more social-educational equality male babies were murder relatively less often and female babies were murdered relatively more often. [The index of social-educational equality was unrelated to the overall homicide rate ($r = -0.01$), the homicide rate for babies ($r = 0.10$), or the male/female ratio for the overall homicide rate ($r = -0.05$).]

Level of Economic Activity

To explore the effects of economic activity, the gross national product per capita for the nations was obtained from the Bureau of the Census (1971). The overall homicide rate was negatively related to the gnp per capita ($r = -0.39$, $p = .017$), but the murder rate for babies was not ($r = 0.11$). However, the sex ratio for babies murdered was negatively related to the gnp per capita (r = -0.45, p = .008) as was the sex ratio for the overall homicide rate (r = -0.59, p < .001).

DISCUSSION

The present study identified several important associations. First, the rate with which babies are murdered in nations of the world is unrelated to the overall homicide rates in those nations. Rather, the murder of babies is more common where the suicide rate is high. This conclusion replicates an earlier report by Lester (1974) and suggests that the murder of babies is associated with self-destructive impulses rather than homicidal impulses.

The murder rate of babies did not appear to be related to indices of female inequality or economic activity. However, the sex ratio for babies murdered was more balanced than the sex ratio for all murder victims, and the proportion of female babies murdered was less in nations where the suicide rate was lower, the overall homicide rate higher, the level of economic activity lower and female equality lower.

Thus, female babies are murdered at a rate more comparable to that of males as the suicide rate goes up, as the overall homicide rate goes down, as the gross national product increases, and as the degree of female equality increases. It looks then as if economic and social progress is accompanied by a more egalitarian victimization for female babies.

REFERENCES

Christoffel, K., Liu, K., & Stamler, J. Epidemiology of fatal child abuse. *Journal of Chronic Diseases*, 1981, 34, 57-64.

Bureau of the Census. *Statistical Abstract of the United States, 1969*. Washington, DC: US Government Printing Office, 1971.

Lester, D. A cross-national study of suicide and homicide. *Behavior Science Research*, 1974, 9, 307-318.

Lester, D. The distribution of sex and age among victims of homicide. *International Journal of Social Psychiatry*, 1986, 32(2), 47-50.

Lester, D. Murdering babies. *Social Psychiatry & Psychiatric Epidemiology*, 1991, 26, 83-85.

Resnick, P. J. Child murder by parents. *American Journal of Psychiatry*, 1969, 126, 325-334.

Stewart, A. J., & Winter, D. G. The nature and causes of female suppression. *Signs*, 1977, 2, 531-553.

CHAPTER 16

TIME-SERIES ANALYSES, 1950-1985

The present book has been concerned primarily with regional studies of the suicide and homicide rates. What predicts the variation in suicide and homicide rates from nation to nation? The present chapter explores instead the variation in suicide and homicide rates over time within nations.

Two major sets of predictors are explored. First, based on Durkheim's (1897) theory of suicide, measures of domestic social integration are used to predict time-series suicide and homicide rates (marriage, birth and divorce rates). Second, based on empirical research (Platt, 1984), unemployment is explored as a predictor of time-series suicide and homicide rates.

Previous research on this issue has studied only one or two nations, and used different time periods, different measures of divorce and other variables, different statistical packages and different sets of variables in the multiple regression analyses. For example, Yang, et al. (1992) used the divorce rate, Lester and Yang (1991) used the ratio of divorces to marriages, while Stack (1990) used the number of divorces divided by the numbers of divorces plus marriages.

It would be of great interest to use standardized time periods, sets of variables, and statistical techniques to examine the reliability of the associations between suicide rates and domestic integration over time in nations of the world. The present study was designed to do this for a set of nations with available data.

Method

Data on suicide and homicide rates from 1950 to 1985 were obtained from the World Health Organization (annual). However, some of the nations in the sample had missing data for one or more years. The author obtained data for the missing years by writing to suicidologists in those nations to obtain xeroxed copies of official government tables of suicide rates.

Choice of the independent variables was limited by the difficulty of obtaining 35 years of continuous data. Few nations can provide such long-term time-series data on social indicators. The three measures of domestic integration used were the crude marriage, divorce and birth rates, obtained from the United Nations (annual). This data set was used since it is easily obtainable by other investigators wishing to replicate the present study and because use of a single data source ensures some standardization of the data. Unemployment rates were obtained from the International Labour Office (annual).

The time series regressions were carried using a statistical package from Doan (1990), with the Cochrane-Orcutt method to correct for serial autocorrelation which was present in many of the national data sets.

Results

Suicide and Domestic Integration

The results of the time-series regressions are shown in Table 16.1. It can be seen that the majority of the regression coefficients for the marriage rate were negative (20 out of 27, $X^2 = 6.16$, df = 1, $p < .02$), indicating that higher marriage rates are typically associated with lower suicide rates as predicted by Durkheim. Six of these regression coefficients were negative and statistically significant while none was positive and statistically significant (one-tailed binomial $p = .016$), confirming the above conclusion.

For divorce rates, 20 of the regression coefficients were positive and 7 were negative ($p < .02$), indicating that higher divorce rates are typically associated with higher suicide rates as predicted by Durkheim. Ten of the

Table 16.1

Results Of The Multivariate Time-Series Regressions For 27 Nations

	constant	marriage rate	birth rate	divorce rate	R^2	Durbin-Watson statistic
Australia	8.928	0.004	0.189	-0.181	0.69	1.78
Austria	11.787**	-0.150	0.219	6.967***	0.81	2.03
Belgium	19.050	-0.869	-0.076	5.476*	0.95	1.89
Canada	10.796***	0.130	-0.192***	1.961***	0.98	1.56
Czechoslov.	28.449***	0.382	-0.327	-2.649	0.79	2.36
Denmark	23.383	-0.251	-0.363	3.410	0.84	2.01
England/Wales	8.434**	-0.653*	0.390**	-0.043	0.95	1.30
Finland	19.639**	-0.137	-0.075	3.487*	0.86	2.16
France	12.078**	-1.068**	0.437*	4.872***	0.95	2.28
Hungary	49.455**	-0.550	-0.213	3.204	0.96	2.45
Iceland	27.981	-0.355	-0.469	-2.904	0.20	1.71
Japan	3.126	0.590	-0.249	10.292*	0.86	1.11
Luxembourg#	21.666**	-1.113	-0.284	3.651	0.69	1.90
Mexico	1.418	-0.084	0.018	-0.121	0.27	2.01
Netherlands	5.286	0.036	-0.021	2.712***	0.96	1.62
New Zealand	11.322***	-0.282	-0.010	0.632	0.49	1.97
N. Ireland	-1.602	-0.352	0.373*	4.721***	0.65	2.13
Norway	0.242	-0.738**	0.462	6.323***	0.96	1.93
Portugal##	8.424***	-0.217	0.100	1.134	0.34	2.02
Puerto Rico	2.104	-0.078	0.273*	0.407	0.65	2.06
Scotland	6.653	-0.051	0.083	1.008	0.83	1.98
Sweden	12.078*	-1.076	0.968*	0.337	0.58	2.03
Switzerland	15.412	0.924	-0.488	5.357	0.90	2.06
Taiwan	2.040	0.205	0.266*	2.649	0.80	2.10
USA	16.310***	-0.368**	-0.151***	0.430***	0.92	2.08
West Germany	26.757***	-0.754*	-0.038	-0.359	0.80	1.87
Yugoslavia	32.110***	-1.175***	-0.242***	-3.701***	0.93	1.28
positive		7	12	20		
negative		20	15	7		
significant & positive		0	6	10		
significant & negative		6	3	1		

\# interpolation used for one year of missing suicide rates
\## interpolation used for three years of missing suicide rates

*** p < .001
** p < .01
* p < .05

positive regression coefficients were statistically significant while only one of the negative coefficients was statistically significant (one-tailed binomial $p = .006$).

For the birth rate, however, 12 of the regression coefficients were positive (6 significantly so) and 15 were negative (3 significantly so), indicating no significant trend.

To explore correlates of the sign of the regression coefficients (positive versus negative), point-biserial correlation coefficients were calculated between the sign of the regresssion coefficient (negative coded as zero and positive as one) and the suicide, marriage, birth and divorce rates of the nations in 1950 and, in addition, the real gross domestic product per capita in 1950 obtained from Summers and Heston (1984). None of these variables was associated with the sign of the regression coefficients for marriage or divorce rates. However, the sign of the regression coefficient for birth rates was associated with 1950 marriage rates ($r = -0.47$, two-tailed $p = .012$). Nations with a negative regression coefficient for birth rates (as predicted by Durkheim's theory) had significantly higher marriage rates in 1950 than nations with a positive regression coefficient. Thus, Durkheim's theory as it pertains to societal birth rates was supported in nations where the marriage rate was relatively higher.

SUICIDE, MARRIAGE AND BIRTH RATES

Several nations either do not report divorce rates consistently or do not permit divorce, and so divorce rates are unavailable. The analyses were run, therefore, just for marriage and birth rates so that these nations could be included.

The results of the regression analyses of the time series data sets are shown in Table 16.2. For marriage rates, it can be seen that, the regression coefficient was negative for 22 of the 33 nations ($X^2 = 3.67$, $df = 1$, ns). Of those statistically significant, however, seven out of seven were negative (binomial $p = .008$). Thus, there is a trend for the higher the marriage rate in a nation, the lower the suicide rate.

Table 16.2

Results Of The Regression Analyses For Marriage And Birth On Suicide For 33 Nations

(b coefficients are shown)

	constant	marriage rate	birth rate	R^2	Durbin-Watson statistic
Australia	8.19	-0.09	0.25	0.69	1.78
Austria	29.24***	0.02	-0.36	0.69	2.19
Belgium	45.52***	-2.05*	-0.97***	0.94	1.71
Canada	16.39**	0.04	-0.24	0.97	1.45
Chile#	7.78*	-0.25	0.01	0.36	1.49
Czechoslov.	25.00***	0.18	-0.33	0.77	2.39
Denmark	40.92***	-1.53	-0.47	0.82	2.07
England/Wales	8.29**	-0.66*	0.39**	0.95	1.31
Finland	35.99***	-0.67	-0.55***	0.83	1.97
France	151.38*	-0.91	0.39	0.93	2.41
Hungary	70.47**	0.14	-0.46	0.96	2.48
Iceland	15.62*	-0.06	-0.19	0.18	1.68
Ireland	14.42*	0.12	-0.36	0.89	2.42
Italy	10.41	-0.51	-0.04	0.59	2.00
Japan	18.17**	0.36	-0.20	0.84	1.20
Liechtenstein	24.36	-0.31	-0.51	0.03	1.91
Luxembourg#	35.60***	-2.11*	-0.61	0.67	1.95
Mexico	1.36	-0.08	0.02	0.27	2.02
Netherlands	17.11***	-0.39	-0.34***	0.94	1.50
New Zealand	15.05***	-0.34	-0.12**	0.43	2.04
N. Ireland	9.34	-0.90	0.11	0.57	2.20
Norway	25.83***	-0.96*	-0.64**	0.94	1.99
Portugal###	10.30***	-0.21	0.02	0.32	2.02
Puerto Rico	4.18	0.02	0.21***	0.64	2.07
Scotland	8.64	0.36	0.13	0.83	2.07
Singapore	8.76*	0.12	0.01	0.03	1.80
Spain##	8.00***	-0.23	-0.08	0.88	1.11
Sweden	13.73***	-1.11*	0.90*	0.58	2.05
Switzerland	31.59***	0.69	-1.02**	0.89	1.95
Taiwan	4.11	0.22	0.24*	0.79	2.05
USA	19.58***	-0.32	-0.27***	0.90	1.89
West Germany	25.81***	-0.73*	-0.01	0.79	1.85
Yugoslavia	27.50***	-1.11***	-0.24***	0.89	1.54

\# interpolation used for one year of missing suicide rates
\## interpolation used for two years of missing suicide rates
\### interpolation used for three years of missing suicide rates

* $p < .05$
** $p < .01$
*** $p < .001$

For birth rates, the regression coefficient was negative for 21 of the 33 nations (ns). Of those statistically significant, eight were negative and four positive (binomial $p = .19$). Clearly the effect of the birth rate on the suicide rate was weaker than the effect of the marriage rate.

The multiple R^2 values ranged from 0.03 for Liechtenstein and Singapore to 0.97 for Canada, with a median value of 0.79, indicating that, in general, these two predictor variables (the marriage and birth rates) were quite successful in predicting the suicide rate.

MULTICOLLINEARITY

To explore the effect of multicollinearity in the independent variables, the Pearson correlations between each of the independent and dependent variables are shown in Table 16.3, and the results of bivariate time series regressions for each independent variable regressed alone on the suicide rate are shown in Table 16.4.

It can be seen in Table 16.3 that marriage and birth rates, marriage and divorce rates and birth and divorce rates were consistently associated in the sample of nations. Interestingly, however, some deviations appeared. In the USA, the correlation between marriage and birth rates was negative, not positive, and the correlation between marriage and divorce rates positive, not negative, possibly due to the high rate of remarriage in the USA.

The Pearson correlations indicated negative correlations between both the marriage and birth rates and the suicide rate and a positive correlation between the divorce rate and the suicide rate. Again, there were exceptions to this (for example, in Australia and England/Wales), and not all of the associations were statistically significant.

The results of the bivariate regressions of each independent variable alone on the suicide rate are shown in Table 16.4. It can be seen that the marriage rate and the suicide rate were significantly associated in only six of the 33 nations, whereas the positive association between the divorce rate and the suicide rate was statistically significant and positive in 13 nations and negative in one nation. The birth rate and the suicide rate were

Table 16.3

Pearson Correlations Between The Suicide And Measures Of Domestic Integration

	marriage & birth	marriage & divorce	divorce & birth	suicide & marriage	suicide & birth	suicide & divorce
Australia	0.37*	-0.39*	-0.87*	0.04	0.04	-0.30
Austria	0.79*	-0.62*	-0.83*	-0.55*	-0.65*	0.87*
Belgium	0.53*	-0.73*	-0.92*	-0.78*	-0.84*	0.95
Canada	-0.07	0.01	-0.86*	0.06	-0.93*	0.97*
Chile	0.20	-	-	-0.17	-0.01	-
Czechoslov.	0.55*	0.10	-0.42*	0.17	-0.41*	0.12
Denmark	0.93*	-0.93*	-0.90*	-0.81*	-0.77*	0.81*
England/Wales	0.43*	-0.49*	-0.87*	-0.01	0.74*	-0.80*
Finland	0.46*	-0.65*	-0.85*	-0.63*	-0.87*	0.85*
France	0.59*	-0.77*	-0.83*	-0.90*	-0.63*	0.89*
Hungary	0.83*	-0.65*	-0.66*	-0.68*	-0.58*	0.94*
Iceland	0.62*	-0.70*	-0.92*	-0.15	-0.21	0.14
Ireland	0.46*	-	-	-0.02	-0.66*	-
Italy	0.95*	-	-	-0.65*	-0.60*	-
Japan	0.47*	-0.78*	-0.54*	-0.31	0.05	-0.07
Liechtenstein	-0.56*	-	-	-0.01	-0.14	-
Luxembourg	0.65*	-0.77*	-0.80*	-0.68*	-0.71*	0.80*
Mexico	-0.09	-0.24	0.30	-0.22	0.45*	0.05
Netherlands	0.75*	-0.86*	-0.94*	-0.82*	-0.94*	0.97*
New Zealand	0.41*	-0.41*	-0.88*	-0.42*	-0.62*	0.68*
N. Ireland	0.48*	-0.39*	-0.72*	-0.13	-0.18	0.66
Norway	0.88*	-0.82*	-0.98*	-0.86*	-0.95*	0.97*
Portugal	0.17	-0.25	-0.85*	-0.42*	0.16	0.04
Puerto Rico	-0.61*	0.74*	-0.93*	-0.44*	0.78*	-0.69*
Scotland	0.67*	-0.78*	-0.92*	-0.68*	-0.51*	0.71*
Singapore	-0.95*	-	-	0.02	-0.01	-
Spain	0.91*	-	-	-0.13	-0.15	-
Sweden	0.91*	-0.83*	-0.80*	-0.35*	-0.20	0.27
Switzerland	0.95*	-0.93*	-0.96*	-0.63*	-0.75*	0.77*
Taiwan	0.03	0.42*	-0.45*	-0.41*	0.63*	-0.35*
USA	-0.63*	0.66*	-0.88*	0.56*	-0.90*	0.90
West Germany	0.89*	-0.63*	-0.74*	-0.86*	-0.77*	0.52*
Yugoslavia	0.88*	-0.13	-0.15	-0.88*	-0.91*	-0.03

* two-tailed p = .05 or better

significantly associated negatively in 11 nations and positively in three nations. Thus, birth and divorce rates appear to be more strongly associated with the suicide rate than marriage rates.

Table 16.4

Results Of the Linear Regressions Of Each Measure Of Domestic Integration Alone On The Suicide Rate
(b coefficients shown, correcting for serial autocorrelation)

	marriage	birth	divorce
Australia	0.115	0.241	-0.307
Austria	0.106	-0.357	5.633***
Belgium	-0.420	-0.209	6.514***
Canada	0.382	-0.252	1.743**
Chile	-0.254	-0.058	-
Czechoslov.	0.129	-0.314	-2.390
Denmark	-2.422***	-0.989***	4.829***
England/Wales	-0.573	0.358*	-0.542
Finland	-0.222	-0.552**	3.946***
France	-0.709	0.276	4.810***
Hungary	-0.033	-0.442	2.759
Iceland	-0.442	-0.198	0.712
Ireland	-0.082	-0.335	-
Italy	-0.629**	-0.193**	-
Japan	0.162	-0.176	8.389
Liechtenstein	0.001	-0.362	-
Luxembourg	-3.028***	-1.236**	6.365***
Mexico	-0.063	0.017	0.110
Netherlands	-0.133	-0.416***	2.766***
New Zealand	-0.645	-0.141**	0.750***
Northern Ireland	-0.817	-0.014	2.988**
Norway	-0.973*	-0.987***	5.225***
Portugal	-0.173	-0.014	0.600
Puerto Rico	-0.207	0.210***	-0.822**
Scotland	0.311	0.110	0.803
Singapore	0.075	-0.021	-
Spain	-0.290	-0.119	-
Sweden	-0.120	0.336	0.014
Switzerland	-0.764	-0.815***	6.768***
Taiwan	0.421	0.242**	1.176
USA	0.034	-0.218***	0.689***
West Germany	-0.763***	-0.257**	-0.276
Yugoslavia	-2.002***	-0.398***	-1.902

HOMICIDE AND DOMESTIC INTEGRATION

The results for homicide are shown in Table 16.5. For divorce rates, it can be seen that 14 of the regression coefficients were positive and four negative (two-tailed binomial p = 0.030). The data for Hungary for 1956 include those killed in the 1956 revolution. Using interpolation for the homicide rate for 1956[14], 15 of the regression coefficients were now positive and three negative (two-tailed binomial p = 0.008). All eight of the regression coefficients reaching statistical significance were positive (two-tailed binomial p = 0.008).

14 the average of the rates for 1955 and 1957.

Table 16.5

Regression Coefficients For Time-Series Analyses Of Homicide Rates, 1950-1985

	constant	marriage	birth	divorce	R^2	Durbin-Watson
Australia	1.953*	0.013	-0.032	0.125*	0.79	1.94
Belgium	3.359	-0.188	-0.086	0.233	0.84	1.85
Canada	1.244	0.120	-0.041*	0.327*	0.94	2.26
England/Wales	-0.081	0.107	-0.016	0.109	0.67	2.14
Finland	-1.393	0.053	0.121*	1.178*	0.48	2.00
France	5.766	-0.441	-0.057	-0.756	0.06	2.01
Hungary	9.445	-1.212	0.511	-1.589	0.08	1.99
Hungary#	2.578	-0.096	0.082	0.894*	0.50	1.74
Iceland	-6.509*	0.297	0.121	1.830*	0.23	2.07
Japan+	-9.550*	0.028	-0.005	0.754	0.96	1.76
Netherlands	1.038*	0.010	-0.042*	0.137*	0.95	2.04
New Zealand	3.241*	-0.092	-0.061*	-0.025	0.54	1.90
N. Ireland	58.191*	-2.524*	-1.755*	-5.510	0.86	1.94
Norway	0.402	-0.004	-0.004	0.352	0.73	1.91
Puerto Rico	-10.032	-4.186	1.393	10.017	0.03	2.02
Sweden	0.729	-0.080	0.018	0.243*	0.81	2.00
USA	0.913	0.305	-0.051	1.245*	0.97	1.65
West Germany	1.279*	0.030	-0.029	0.183	0.68	2.26
Yugoslavia	-4.934*	0.738*	0.068	0.349	0.87	1.68

* significant at the 5% level or better
\# recalculated using a homicide rate for 1956 which was the average of 1955 and 1957
\+ intepolation used for one year of missing homicide rates

The results for marriage and birth rates were not so clear. For marriage rates, ten were positive and eight negative, while for birth rates six were positive and twelve negative.

The general trend identified for time-series homicide rates is that homicide rates are positively associated with divorce rates. Thus, when divorce rates are higher, homicide rates are also higher. It was predicted from Henry and Short's theory that opposite associations would be found for homicide and suicide rates (see Chapter 5). This was not confirmed here, for divorce rates were positively associated with both homicide and suicide rates in this sample of nations. In addition, marriage rates were negatively associated with suicide rates but not associated with homicide rates. Thus, homicide and suicide rates did not show opposite associations.

Table 16.6

Regression Results For Homicide Rates For Marriage And Birth Rates

	constant	marriage	birth	R^2	Durbin-Watson
Australia	2.998*	-0.005	-0.069*	0.74	1.90
Belgium	4.671*	-0.263*	-0.125*	0.83	1.83
Canada	2.883*	0.074	-0.082*	0.92	2.29
England/Wales	0.711	0.094	-0.050	0.66	2.26
Finland	4.382*	-0.193	-0.022	0.36	2.18
France	1.355	-0.112	0.030	0.60	1.69
Hungary	2.379	-0.960	0.606	0.07	2.00
Hungary#	3.181*	-0.001	-0.391	0.38	2.02
Iceland	1.557	0.085	-0.059	0.06	1.97
Japan+	0.419	0.040	-0.003	0.95	1.78
N. Ireland	49.717*	-2.768*	-1.347*	0.85	1.88
Norway	1.811*	-0.008	-0.068	0.72	1.91
Puerto Rico	14.581	1.122*	-0.543*	0.87	1.52
USA	6.329	0.424	-0.094	0.97	1.32
Yugoslavia	-4.526*	0.737*	0.067	0.87	1.72

* significant at the .05 level or better
\# recalculated using a homicide rate for 1956 which was the average of 1955 and 1957
\+ interpolation used for one year of missing homicide rates

DIVORCE/MARRIAGE RATIOS

As mentioned at the beginning of this chapter, some investigators have suggested using a ratio measure for divorce and marriage rates. To explore the effect of this tactic, the regressions were run for suicide first using the marriage and divorce rates separately in the regression analyses and then using the divorce/marriage rate ratio. The results are shown in Table 16.7, where it can be seen that the results are similar for both sets of analyses. Divorce rates were postively associated with suicide for 20 of the 27 nations, as was the divorce/marriage rate ratio. The R^2 were similar for both sets of analyses, though the general tendency was for R^2 to be a little higher when marriage and divorce rates were used separately (ten higher versus two lower). Thus, the use of the ratio measure does not appear to improve predictive accuracy.

Table 16.7

Predicting Suicide Rates Using Marriage And Divorce Rates
(the regression coefficient for the constant is omitted from the table)

	marriage	divorce	R^2	divorce/marriage	R^2
Australia	0.197	-0.319	0.68	-2.587	0.68
Austria	0.113	5.900*	0.80	21.806*	0.74
Belgium	-0.776	5.873*	0.95	38.050*	0.95
Canada	0.132	1.685*	0.97	15.394*	0.97
Czechoslovakia	0.283	-2.649	0.78	-19.090	0.78
Denmark	-0.719	3.725*	0.83	20.717*	0.83
England/Wales	-0.483	-0.382	0.94	-3.460	0.93
Finland	-0.110	3.841*	0.86	20.621*	0.85
France	-1.034*	3.351*	0.94	23.238*	0.94
Hungary	-0.703	3.592*	0.96	32.447*	0.96
Iceland	-0.378	0.220	0.17	4.970	0.17
Japan	0.348	8.588	0.85	11.769	0.84
Luxembourg	-1.257	4.358*	0.69	32.459*	0.66
Mexico	-0.059	0.071	0.21	0.969	0.21
Netherlands	0.048	2.843*	0.96	14.205*	0.95
New Zealand	-0.286	0.673*	0.49	5.818*	0.49
N. Ireland	-0.406	2.727*	0.61	20.068*	0.61
Norway	-0.579*	4.260*	0.96	24.288*	0.97
Portugal	-0.132	0.359	0.32	4.323	0.31
Puerto Rico	0.045	-0.856*	0.57	-9.127*	0.56
Scotland	0.025	0.799	0.83	5.719	0.83
Sweden	-0.137	-0.068	0.52	0.271	0.52
Switzerland	0.437	7.682*	0.89	26.716*	0.88
Taiwan	0.441	1.843	0.75	-4.059	0.75
USA	-0.247	0.807*	0.88	8.101*	0.88
West Germany	-0.833*	-0.319	0.80	-1.649	0.76
Yugoslavia	-2.162*	-3.237*	0.86	-15.276	0.90

* significant at the 5% level or better

SUICIDE AND UNEMPLOYMENT

The regressions were conducted both with the unemployment rate as the only explanatory variable and with both unemployment and divorce rates as the explanatory variables.

As seen in Table 16.8, the regression coefficient for the unemployment rate alone was significant only for four of the twelve countries, namely, Japan, the Netherlands, Taiwan, and the USA. When the divorce rate was included in the regression, Denmark, Norway, Taiwan and the USA had a significant regression coefficient for the unemployment rate. Among the

Table 16.8

Time-Series Regression Of Suicide On Unemployment

	regression coefficients Unemployment	Constant	R^2	Pearson Correlation
Austria	0.173	24.217***	0.69	0.03
Belgium	0.029	113.705*	0.93	0.71#
Canada	0.110	15.433**	0.97	0.73#
Denmark	-0.032	24.632***	0.77	0.49#
England/Wales	-0.029	8.942***	0.93	-0.53#
Ireland	0.075	16.289	0.89	0.83#
Japan	2.322*	13.860***	0.86	0.24
Netherlands	0.174**	8.244***	0.94	0.86#
Norway	0.174	-3.221	0.94	0.06
Sweden	-0.574	20.509	0.54	-0.21
Taiwan	2.545**	8.782***	0.79	0.73#
USA	0.133*	10.737***	0.86	0.69#
West Germany	0.124	19.969***	0.77	-0.04

	regression coefficients Unemployment	Divorce rate	Constant	R^2
Austria	0.041	5.625***	15.727***	0.80
Belgium	0.101	5.971***	10.717***	0.95
Canada	0.108	1.712**	7.786***	0.97
Denmark	0.382**	4.559***	11.640***	0.84
England/Wales	-0.001	-0.541	10.495***	0.93
Japan	1.834	5.543	7.270	0.86
Netherlands	0.023	2.610***	5.219***	0.96
Norway	0.340*	5.255***	3.046***	0.96
Sweden	-0.575	0.050	20.417	0.54
Taiwan	2.563**	-2.053	9.901***	0.79
USA	0.118*	0.578***	8.604***	0.89
West Germany	0.155	-0.459	20.548***	0.77

* p < .05
** p < .01
*** p < .001
\# two-tailed p < .05 or better

13 countries in the sample, then, only six countries support the positive association between the unemployment rate and the suicide rate. This result supports a countercyclical association, as proposed by Henry and Short (1954), though only in the minority of the nations studied.

HOMICIDE AND UNEMPLOYMENT

Looking at the simple Pearson correlation between homicide and unemployment rates (see Table 16.9), eight of the ten correlations were positive and two were negative (Japan and West Germany). Five of the positive correlations were statistically significant and the negative correlation was also statistically significant.

When time-series multiple regressions were run for unemployment alone (see Table 16.9), six of the ten regression coefficients were positive, though one was statistically significant (surprisingly that for Japan).

Table 16.9

Time-Series Regression Analyses For Homicide On Unemployment

	regression coefficients constant	unemployment	R^2	Pearson Correlation
Belgium	25.934	-0.013	0.80	0.68#
Canada	1.822***	0.041	0.92	0.67#
England/Wales	0.778***	-0.016	0.64	0.29
Ireland	0.038	0.146	0.25	0.40#
Japan	-3.329*	0.199*	0.96	-0.55#
Netherlands	0.572***	0.016	0.91	0.78
Norway	0.733***	-0.015	0.69	0.34#
Sweden	1.033***	-0.024	0.63	0.30
USA	10.375**	0.019	0.96	0.54#
West Germany	1.112***	0.008	0.64	-0.07

	regression coefficients			R^2
	constant	unemployment	divorce	
Belgium	0.315**	0.003	0.712***	0.83
Canada	1.113***	0.029	0.386**	0.93
England/Wales	0.477***	-0.057**	0.264***	0.71
Japan	-18.122**	0.163	0.482	0.96
Netherlands	0.108**	-0.016*	0.459***	0.93
Norway	0.308	-0.014	0.382*	0.73
Sweden	0.266**	0.042	0.319	0.77
USA	1.472	0.032	1.517***	0.97
West Germany	1.060***	0.003	0.052	0.64

* two-tailed p < .05
** two-tailed p < .01
*** two-tailed p < .001
\# two-tailed p < .05 or better

Time-series regressions were also run including divorce rates as well, since earlier preliminary research had indicated that divorce rates were a consistent contributor to multiple regressions on homicide rates. As expected, all nine of the regression coefficients for divorce were positive, and six were statically significant. However, for unemployment rates, six of the nine regression coefficients were positive and three negative, but only the regression coefficients for England/Wales and the Netherlands were statistically significant, both negative.

The results of this study, therefore, provide little support for an association of unemployment rates with homicide rates in the ten nations studied. Although the simple correlation coefficients were positive on the whole, as predicted, more complex time-series multiple regression analysis failed to confirm this positive association. Thus, it must be concluded that unemployment and homicide rates are not associated in nations of the world.

Discussion

The present study used standardized time-periods, data sets, variable definitions, and regression techiques to explore the validity of Durkheim's theory relating domestic integration to suicide in twenty-one nations. The results indicated good agreement with predictions for marriage and divorce rates, but poor agreement for birth rates. However, support for the predictions regarding marriage and divorce rates was not obtained in every nation studied.

Thus, this study shows the importance of cross-cultural replication of studies in order to provide some idea of the generalizability of the results reported. Studies of merely one or two nations are not sufficient to provide this information.

Once a study such as the present one has been conducted, research can then move to the next question, namely under what conditions are the predicted associations obtained. The present study provided some answers for the effect of birth rates on suicide. The predicted effect (a negative association as predicted by Durkheim) was found in nations with higher marriage rates. This enables us to speculate that, perhaps, the beneficial impact of children with respect to suicidal behavior is found only in nations with relatively higher marriage rates. This, of course, generates further questions, namely the mechanisms by which this might operate.

It should also be noted that suicide rates vary greatly *within* some nations and that not every region may show the same pattern. For example, in Canada, time-series analyses of the suicide rate in Quebec do not always produce the same results as similar analyses in other provinces (Cormier and Klerman, 1985). In the present study, separate analyses were run for the three regions in the United Kingdom (England/Wales, Scotland, and Northern Ireland) since the British government typically reports statistics for these three regions separately. Conducting separate analyses for the different regions in other nations may also be fruitful.

It is clear, therefore, that the results of the present study are stimulating for future research.

References

Cormier, H. J., & Klerman, G. L. Unemployment and male-female labor force participation as determinants of changing suicide rates of males and females in Quebec. *Social Psychiatry*, 1985, 20, 109-114.

Doan, T. A. *Regression analysis of time series*. Evanston, IL: Var Econometrics, 1990.

Durkheim, E. *Le suicide*. Paris: Felix Alcan, 1897.

Henry, A. F., & Short, J. F. *Suicide and Homicide*, New York: Free Press, 1954.

International Labour Office. *Year book of labour statistics*. Geneva, Switzerland: International Labour Office, annual.

Lester, D., & Yang, B. The relationship between divorce, unemployment and female participation in the labour force and suicide rates in Australia and America. *Australian & New Zealand Journal of Psychiatry*, 1991, 25, 519-523.

Platt, S. D. Unemployment and suicidal behavior. *Social Science and Medicine*, 1984, 19, 93-115.

Stack, S. The effect of divorce on suicide in Denmark, 1951-1980. *Sociological Quarterly*, 1990, 31, 359-370.

Summers, R., & Heston, A. Improved international comparisons of real product and its composition. *Review of Income and Wealth*, 1984, 30, 207-262.

United Nations. *Demographic Yearbook.* New York: United Nations, annual.

World Health Organization. *Statistics Annual.* Geneva, Switzerland: World Health Organization, annual.

Yang, B., Lester, D., & Yang, C. H. Sociological and economic theories of suicide. *Social Science & Medicine,* 1992, 34, 333-334.

Chapter 17

Conclusions

This volume has endeavored to collect data on suicide rate and homicide rates for as large a sample of nations as possible and to explore social correlates of these rates. These rates have been published here as a resource for other investigators. It seems unlikely that as large a sample will be possible for more recent times. Overall, fewer nations are reporting mortality statistics to the World Health Organization, and national governments are often unwilling to respond to requests for data. On the other hand, a few nations are reporting mortality statistics, and especially suicide and homicide rates, for the first time, such as Russia and Rumania.

The evidence available indicated that the official suicide rates reported by nations have a fair measure of reliability and validity despite differences in the way in which suicidal and homicidal deaths are investigated and counted in different nations. In addition, national suicide rates do appear to be reasonably stable from year to year, meeting one of the conditions for meaningful study.

A large number of social correlates were identified both for national suicide rates and for national homicide rates. Furthermore, the correlations were in opposite directions for suicide and homicide, confirming the theory proposed by Henry and Short that social conditions have opposite effects on suicide and homicide. Social conditions which are associated with an increase in the suicide rate are associated with a decrease in the homicide rate, and vice versa.

A factor analysis of the social variables identified six clusters of variables, only one of which was associated with rates of personal violence.

Suicide rates were associated positively with an index of social disintegration while homicide rates were associated negatively with this index. In addition, the quality of life in nations was found to be very strong predictor of both suicide and homicide rates.

Although the study was successful in finding social variables which correlated with the national suicide and homicide rates, it was less successful in identifying social correlates of changes in these rates over a decade. More thought needs to be given, both to theory and empirical study, in order to identify correlates of changes in the rates of personal violence.

Several trends were identified in suicide and homicide, both in the rates and in the methods used in recent years. Differences by age were large, while differences by gender were relatively small. It was also noted that the murder rates for babies were more strongly associated with national suicide rates than with national homicide rates.

A critical-mass theory of suicide, namely that, as a behavior becomes more common in a society, its rate begins to rise monotonically, was found to hold true for the 1970s, but not for the 1980s. There appears to be a general trend for suicide rates to have peaked in many nations around 1980 and to be declining a little in recent years.

Finally, time-series analyses were presented for 33 nations, examining predictors of the annual suicide and homicide rates from 1950 to 1985. Hitherto, published research papers have considered only one nation at a time, and so it has been difficult to ascertain which results are generalizable to other nations and which are unique to the nation being studied. The present analyses identified trends which seem to hold true for most nations, such as the association between suicide and homicide rates.

In summary, it is hoped that the raw data presented in this volume will be of use to other investigators of personal violence and that the hypotheses tested will stimulate others to propose alternative theories and seek new strategies for examining their usefulness in explaining the national variation in rates of suicide and homicide.

Subject Index

Adults, 116
Afghanistan, 18, 36
Africa, 18, 19, 22, 24, 34, 35, 36, 39, 41, 42, 88, 129
age-standardized rates, 7, 8
aggression, 65, 67, 70
Agriculture, 46, 57, 67
alcohol, 3, 46, 47, 49, 51, 52, 53, 54, 56, 61, 66, 69, 92, 94, 111, 112, 116, 117
Algeria, 18, 36
America, 4, 17, 19, 34, 40, 41, 51, 53, 56, 57, 70, 84, 102, 104, 118, 157
American Samoa, 33
Anglos, 16, 17
Angola, 33, 36
Antigua, 32
area, 60, 66, 69, 116
Argentina, 28, 31, 37, 82, 83, 98, 100
Asia, 18, 19, 34, 39, 41, 84, 88, 118
attempted murder, 12
Australasia, 37
Australia, 9, 10, 13, 14, 16, 22, 23, 24, 26, 28, 31, 37, 40, 76, 77, 78, 79, 82, 83, 88, 91, 92, 98, 104, 106, 113, 115, 116, 118, 120, 121, 131, 136, 143, 145, 147, 148, 149, 150, 151, 157
Austria, 8, 9, 10, 13, 15, 20, 21, 22, 26, 28, 31, 38, 40, 69, 77, 82, 83, 88, 91, 92, 98, 100, 104, 106, 113, 112, 115, 116, 118, 120, 121, 131, 136, 143, 145, 147, 148, 151
Bahamas, 13, 31, 33
Bangladesh, 36
Barbados, 13, 28, 31
Belgium, 8, 20, 21, 22, 28, 31, 38, 40, 69, 77, 78, 82, 83, 88, 98, 104, 120, 126, 131, 136, 143, 145, 147, 148, 149, 150, 151, 152, 153
Belize, 31, 33
Benin, 36
Bermuda, 32, 33
Bhutan, 36
birth rate, 60, 66, 69, 72, 94, 113, 116
Blacks, 18
Bolivia, 37
Brazil, 25, 26, 31, 37, 69, 77, 82, 88
Bulgaria, 8, 9, 10, 19, 26, 28, 31, 38, 40, 69, 82, 83, 91, 92, 98, 100, 104, 106, 112, 113, 115, 116, 118, 120, 121, 126, 136
Burkina Faso, 36

Burma, 36
Burundi, 33
caloric intake, 47, 50, 52, 54, 55, 61, 66, 68, 69, 85, 86, 111, 112
Cameroon, 36
Canada, 8, 9, 10, 13, 15, 26, 28, 31, 37, 40, 69, 77, 78, 82, 83, 88, 90, 91, 92, 94, 98, 100, 104, 106, 113, 115, 116, 118, 120, 121, 131, 136, 143, 145, 147, 148, 149, 150, 151, 152, 153, 157
Canal Zone, 33
Cape Verde, 31, 33
Cayman Islands, 31, 33
Central Africa, 36
Chad, 36
Channel Islands, 33
child labor, 66
children, 72, 112, 113, 156
Chile, 8, 9, 10, 13, 26, 28, 31, 37, 40, 69, 82, 83, 91, 92, 98, 104, 111, 113, 115, 118, 120, 136, 145, 147, 148, 149
China, 18, 36
Chinese, 17, 19
Christians, 46, 48, 49, 60, 66, 68, 85
cities, 68
civil liberties, 45, 48, 66, 69, 112
colored, 18
Columbia, 28, 32, 37, 69, 98
Congo, 36
Cook Islands, 32, 33
corn consumption, 66
Coroner's Decisions, 11
Costa Rica, 13, 26, 28, 31, 33, 37, 40, 69, 77, 82, 83, 98, 113, 120, 126, 136
Cuba, 28, 33, 37, 104, 120, 136
cultural diversity, 128, 129, 130, 131
cutting, 77, 79, 89
Czechoslovakia, 15, 28, 31, 38, 40, 69, 82, 83, 98, 100, 104, 120, 136, 143, 145, 147, 148, 151
death rate, 60, 66, 113, 116
defense effort, 128, 129, 130, 131
defense expenditure, 66, 69
demography, 128, 129, 130, 131
Denmark, 1, 8, 12, 13, 20, 21, 22, 26, 28, 31, 38, 40, 69, 77, 78, 82, 83, 88, 91, 92, 98, 100, 101, 104, 106, 113, 115, 118, 120, 121, 131, 136, 143, 145, 147, 148, 151, 152, 153, 157

UK, 8, 9, 10, 12, 13, 15, 22, 27, 32, 33, 38, 41, 69, 82, 83, 98, 108, 115, 123, 136
UK Virgin Islands, 30, 32, 33
under fifteen, 66, 69
under-developed nations, 42
unemployment rate, 46, 48, 51, 153, 154, 156
unemployment, 46, 48, 51, 55, 66, 68, 113, 143, 153, 154, 156, 157
unionization, 66, 69
United Arab Republic, 37
United States, 32, 33, 102, 111, 116, 141
urban, 68, 69, 113, 116
urban growth, 66, 69
Uruguay, 29, 33, 37, 120, 136, 194
urban population, 45, 46, 47, 48, 60, 62, 68, 71, 72, 86, 112, 117
USA, 8, 9, 10, 12, 13, 15, 16, 17, 18, 20, 21, 22, 23, 27, 37, 40, 69, 75, 76, 77, 78, 82, 83, 91, 92, 94, 98, 101, 104, 109, 111, 113, 115, 118, 120, 123, 129, 131, 136, 143, 145, 147, 148, 149, 150, 151, 152, 153
USSR, 15, 38, 69
Venezuela, 13, 25, 27, 32, 33, 37, 40, 69, 77, 78, 82, 83, 98, 104, 111, 113, 115, 118, 120, 136
Violence, 65, 68, 84
Wallis Island, 29
Wars, 51
weight, 66, 69
welfare effort, 128, 129, 130, 131
Western Samoa, 29
whites, 17, 18, 129
women, 46, 51, 68, 83, 86, 87, 88, 90, 92, 94, 111, 112, 113, 115, 119, 120, 131, 140
women's status, 128, 129, 130, 131
World Health Organization, 7, 10, 11, 12, 13, 14, 15, 20, 23, 24, 25, 26, 75, 79, 90, 92, 99, 106, 117, 135, 144, 158, 159
young, 116
Yugoslavia, 29, 32, 33, 38, 69, 77, 82, 83, 98, 113, 143, 145, 147, 148, 149, 150, 151, 152
Zaire, 36
Zambia, 18, 24
Zimbabwe, 18, 24, 30, 34, 36, 39, 69, 82, 83, 98